The Southampton Arms

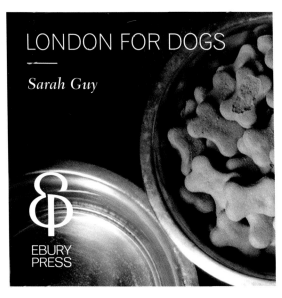

LONDON FOR DOGS

Sarah Guy

EBURY
PRESS

Epping Forest

Hyde Park

Urban life can be tough, but London has lots to offer a dog. Featured here are places and events that make the city fun for hound and owner, from pro-dog department stores to fox-scented woods. Read on for all types and sizes of parks; well-stocked, interesting shops with knowledgeable staff; and every sort of dog-friendly hangout, whether you want a morning coffee stop or a glamorous restaurant. Turn what could be a stressful trip to the centre of town into a welcome jaunt with the right combination of café and green space. Or discover a wild walk only a tube ride away – London has an amazing number of accessible acres, even in the most built-up areas.

As London becomes increasingly dog-friendly, events, meet-ups and dog shows are popping up all over the place. Most parks function as community hubs where dog walkers meet on a daily basis, and where more organised get-togethers happen at weekends. Parks have more varied terrain these days, too, providing stretches of long grass as well as manicured lawns, and plenty of untamed undergrowth to snuffle around in. You'll find the best of them here, together with all manner of services, gifts and accessories, walks, and out of town jaunts for canines in need of a change of scene.

Unless it's obvious (a water bowl on the doorstep is a good indicator!) that an establishment welcomes dogs, it is always worth asking if it's OK to cross the threshold. Not only is it polite, but you may find that your small, quiet dog gets admitted where some mutts wouldn't. And though most chains are distinctly dog-phobic, certain branches may exercise leeway, particularly in dog-centric neighbourhoods. Conversely, a firm's pet policy can change at any time (all it takes is a new manager). Take inspiration from the selection that follows, and explore the city with your dog.

Lincoln's Inn Fields

CENTRAL LONDON

The mean streets of any big city are hard on a dog, but London's can be more fun than most. There are so many parks and squares, from the magnificent spread of Hyde Park to delightful enclosed spaces such as Lincoln's Inn Fields. It's also getting easier to have a coffee with your four-legged companion, and to pop into certain shops – dog-loving department store Liberty is the most notable example in the West End. So, while pounding the pavements might not make a dog's day, we've found plenty of places to appease them.

Get a caffeine fix at Fernandez & Wells

Great hangouts for inner-city pooches

———

Usefully dotted around central London, F&W coffee shops can be found in Soho, Mayfair, South Kensington and Somerset House, as well as here, just behind St Giles church. This branch has plenty of space for dogs, and segues into a wine bar in the evenings. All-day food has a Spanish bent; there are cheeses and cured meats, a few cooked dishes (including a mean shakshuka), and plenty of attractively stuffed sandwiches. Coffee is roasted by Has Bean. Service is friendly, and there's a relaxed vibe at odds with the location. Providing your dog isn't driven wild by the smell of cooking chorizo, this is a great place for you both to catch your breath.

fernandezandwells.com
1–3 Denmark Street, WC2H 8LP
Tottenham Court Road tube

Strut your stuff in Liberty

Furry fashionistas are welcome at this famous store

———

Although in theory there's a limit to the size of dog welcome here, in practice any well-behaved pooch is ushered through the doors. There are five floors of fashion, beauty, furniture and household goods to explore in this iconic department store; splash out on a deluxe collar for the hound (available on the ground floor) while you're there. The café is a good bet for afternoon tea, and is as hound-happy as the rest of Liberty.

liberty.co.uk
Regent Street, W1B 5AH
Oxford Circus tube

Fernandez & Wells

Anthropologie, *across the city*
The last word in offbeat chic, this American clothing and homeware store has branches on the King's Road, Marylebone, Regent Street and in Spitalfields. *anthropologie.com/uk*

Apple Store, *Covent Garden Piazza & Regent Street*
Browse the bright white technology – or queue for your appointment – with your pooch by your side. *apple.com/uk*

Aria, *Islington*
See if your dog matches the furniture at this fashionable homeware store. *ariashop.co.uk*

Conran Shop, *Fulham Road & Marylebone High Street*
A long-established arbiter of household taste, from soaps to sofas. Pooches are welcome everywhere, including the Marylebone store's café, Conran Kitchen. *conranshop.co.uk*

Daunt Books, *across the city*
Great browsing, made even better by your hound at your side. Daunt Books have dog-friendly staff and a relaxed atmosphere. *dauntbooks.co.uk*

Farmers' Markets, *across the city*
Simply the best way to food shop with your four-legged friend, and meet like-minded owners. Favourites include those at Blackheath and Alexandra Palace. *lfm.org.uk*

Fenwicks, *New Bond Street*
Browse the fashion here for as long as your faithful companion's patience lasts. *fenwick.co.uk*

Mary's Living & Giving, *across the city*
The luxe charity shop chain (working on behalf of Save the Children) is a dog-friendly zone. *savethechildren.org.uk*

Rough Trade East, *The Old Truman Brewery, Brick Lane*
The much-loved music emporium welcomes well-behaved dogs in the store and the café. Don't hang around for the gigs though. *roughtrade.com*

Selfridges, *Oxford Street*
Dogs that can be carried are welcome in this famous department store. *selfridges.com*

Go walking in Regent's Park
There's something in the air in NW1

The presence of ZSL London Zoo on the northern edge of Regent's Park adds a few extra smells and sounds to an otherwise classic London park. Aside from the ornamental gardens (dogs not allowed) and lakeside (dogs must be on a lead), there's plenty of running around space – particularly if the acres and acres of sports pitches aren't in use. There are lots of cafés and – more useful for dog walkers – coffee kiosks dotted about the park. If you and your four-legged friend want more, extend the walk along Regent's Canal, or cross the canal and stride up Primrose Hill.

royalparks.org.uk
NW1
Baker Street, Camden Town, Great Portland Street, Regent's Park or St John's Wood tube

Make a night of it at the Eagle
Quality food and drink from the original gastropub

This pub is a long-time favourite, and not just with dog owners. Opened in 1991, the Eagle is hailed as the original gastropub, and it's still turning out a menu of simple but effective dishes from a minute kitchen space next to the bar. Options – chalked on a blackboard – change every day, but there's usually a steak sandwich, or you might get lucky and coincide with the Portuguese fish stew. A good range of drinks includes decent wines and plenty of draft beers, plus a tempting Bloody Mary. There's just one simply decorated room (and a few tables on unlovely Farringdon Road), but however busy it gets there's always room for a dog.

theeaglefarringdon.co.uk
159 Farringdon Road, EC1R 3AL
Farringdon tube or rail

St John Bar

Unwind in the St John Bar
Farringdon's temple to modern British food

The main attraction here for dogs is that they might just get a bone from the famous 'nose to tail' kitchen. Their owners are lured in by the easy-going atmosphere and the top-notch British snacks. The Welsh rarebit is a thing of legend, and a fixture on a short seasonal menu that changes daily. Eccles cakes are a popular sweet treat. Bar staff know their business, and thanks to the restaurant upstairs there's a fine choice of French wines. The basic decor – whitewashed walls and simple wooden chairs and tables – means that scruffy mutts won't feel out of place, and the spaciousness allows big dogs sprawling room.

stjohngroup.uk.com
26 St John Street, EC1M 4AY
Barbican tube, or Farringdon tube or rail

Spend some time with Lady Ottoline

A civilised retreat from the Bloomsbury streets

——

An elegant hostelry – just right for its Bloomsbury setting – with a fine range of drinks, especially gins. Here, dogs have to stay on the ground floor (there's a formal restaurant upstairs), either in the bar or at the outdoor tables. You're not missing out, though, as the same menu of upmarket British dishes is served throughout; there's always a roast on Sundays. Settle back with a sloe gin or a bowl of water and enjoy this sanctuary from the hurly-burly.

theladyottoline.com
11A Northington Street, WC1N 2JF
Chancery Lane tube

Have brunch at Ask for Janice

A handy pit stop for dogs who do meetings

——

There's plenty of space at this all-day café, so everyone and their dog can stretch out. The stripped back, industrial-look furnishings mean that no one has to worry about Fido messing the place up, and the cheery demeanour of the staff makes diners and doggies feel wanted. The menu runs from a posh sausage sandwich or avocado on toast through to small plates and full meals. Outside, dogs will sniff the air appreciatively at the smells from nearby Smithfield meat market.

askforjanice.co.uk
50–52 Long Lane, EC1A 9EJ
Barbican tube, or Farringdon tube or rail

Get physical in Hyde Park
Run free in the centre of town

——

A massive 350 acres, Hyde Park is the best place in central London for a big dog – and it runs straight into Kensington Gardens, which adds another 265 acres. There are plenty of areas where dogs can run free; sections of the park where dogs must be on leads, such as the rose garden or around the Serpentine lake, are clearly marked. As well as the impressive formal displays, there are swathes of wild flowers, and big open grassy spaces are mixed in with wooded areas. What it doesn't have is hills, but any dog can still get lots of exercise. Search out the poignant dog cemetery near Bayswater Road (rarely open but you can peep through the railings). Watch out for wildlife, horses and cyclists, and avoid the eastern end of the park during the summer when it becomes a giant concert arena. There are refreshment huts dotted about and two cafés at the Serpentine – dogs permitted outside only. This is a Royal Park, where dog fouling carries a £60 fine, and professional dog walkers must be licensed (they are then listed on the website).

royalparks.org.uk
W2
Hyde Park Corner, Knightsbridge, Lancaster Gate or Marble Arch tube

Hyde Park

Chow down at Shake Shack
Share your burger cravings

—

Dogs are very much considered part of the dining crew at this international burger chain, and the menu includes a couple of 'treats for those with four feet'. The Bag O' Bones consists of red velvet dog biscuits by Bocce's Bakery, while the Pooch-ini is a mix of red velvet dog biscuits, peanut butter sauce and vanilla custard (this gutbuster is not recommended for small dogs). Human choices centre around burgers, hot dogs and frozen custards.

shakeshack.com
24 Market Building, The Piazza, WC2E 8RD
Covent Garden tube

Have a coffee and a bagel at Brill
Sample the Exmouth Market way of life

—

This mellow, café-lined street is actually not that dog-friendly, with the happy exception of Brill. There's a very sunny vibe – staff are lovely – whether you're an adult, child or dog, and there are always good tunes playing in the background. The (own-blend) coffee is worth ordering, and the bagels come fresh from Brick Lane every day; there are also salad and avocado on toast-style options. Perch in the hidden garden at the rear, or in the buzzy interior lined with CDs (for sale), or people-watch from a table looking on to the street. Wherever you sit, you'll no doubt encounter Goose, the charming border terrier from Botanique shop a few doors along, who often wanders in. Keep an eye out for occasional evening openings and music events.

27 Exmouth Market, EC1R 4QL
Angel tube

Shop at Bow Wow London
A dapper dog's delight

—

With goodies ranging from the Dry Dude dog bathrobe to the pheasant-on-a-rope toy, Bow Wow will tempt you into buying things you didn't know your dog needed. There are beautiful, well-made collars, leads, harnesses and bowls, alongside pleasingly daft outfits and dog beauty products. A commitment to ethical, wholesome stock means foodstuffs come from the likes of Natural Instinct, Lily's Kitchen and Billy & Margot. Only you will know if your dog can carry off that sailor's outfit.

bowwowlondon.org
50A Earlham Street, WC2H 9LA
Covent Garden tube

Bow Wow London

MY DOG
Kate Spicer

Locanda Locatelli is a Michelin-starred restaurant round the back of Selfridges. It is, to me, Britain's finest Italian. Certainly, it's the most chic and convivial, with impeccable service. On my birthday, or if someone wants to spoil me, this is usually where I want to go.

When Locanda reopened after a refit in 2015, Roberto, the exuberant general manager, rang and invited me to dinner on him. Oh, what a treat! Not long before, however, I'd adopted Wolfy, a super-chilled Norfolk Lurcher, and I admit I didn't especially want to be parted from him. Roberto talked a little about his terrier, and said, 'The dog is welcome.'

We walked through the David Collins interior, beloved by Gwyneth Paltrow, Madonna and, I remembered, the great painter Lucian Freud. In 2003, I did a short stint – a stage – in the kitchen of Locanda, and I remember when the great painter came in his order would come through without a table number on it, just the words 'FREUD' written across the top. He always sat at the chef's table, sometimes with his whippet.

To my genuine glee, Wolfy and I were directed to the chef's table where I met my friend Elaine, and the three of us sat down for a late lunch. Wolfy has been back many times since, and he

From Locanda Locatelli: whilst dogs are welcome, please let the restaurant know in advance if you are bringing a four-legged friend and make sure they are well-behaved. Dogs can only be accommodated at certain tables due to health and safety.

stretches out on the leather banquette next to me and quietly snoozes. If he's good, Michelin-starred scraps inevitably fall his way.

Eating out in smart restaurants with my dog is one of the most quietly joyful things I do. I was in New York recently, where a dog like Wolfy would never be allowed in a restaurant. I love London for being so much cooler when it comes to me hanging with my dog.

Enjoy being waited on at the Orange
A smart choice for refined drinking and dining

The Orange is the Pimlico outpost of a small chain of upmarket gastropubs, all of which welcome dogs, even big ones. Mutts, from Labs to lapdogs, get a water bowl, while humans choose from the modern European menu – think wood-fired pizzas or the likes of rabbit pie with mash and asparagus. You can get breakfast here too. There's also a bar, decorated in the same low-key stylish way. Staff are friendly and attentive. Other pubs in the group are the Grazing Goat (Marylebone), the Alfred Tennyson (Belgravia) and the Thomas Cubitt (Victoria).

theorange.co.uk
37 Pimlico Road, SW1W 8NE
Sloane Square tube

Kit out a designer dog at Mungo & Maud
For when only the best will do

Describing themselves as 'dog and cat outfitters', Mungo & Maud offers an upmarket range of dog (and cat) accessories, from blankets and bowls to toys and treats. Dog beds come in subtle colours of soft pink and charcoal. There are gifts for humans, too – stationery, bags, jewellery (including an irresistible sausage-dog charm bracelet). It won't surprise you to know that there's also an outlet in Harrods.

mungoandmaud.com
79 Elizabeth Street, SW1W 9PJ
Sloane Square tube

Relish summer at Fields Bar & Kitchen
Enjoy pizza and a beer in Holborn

——

Dogs have to sit outside at this park brasserie, but that's no hardship as that's where the best seats are. Choose between the back terrace overlooking the tennis courts or the area at the front facing the park. Either way, it's hard to believe you're in the centre of town. Lincoln's Inn Fields is a well-run green space, with plenty of shade, and benches dotted about for those who don't want to sit on the grass. It fills up at lunchtime with office workers, but otherwise is pleasantly low-key. The brasserie is run by Benugo; wood-fired pizzas are a speciality, and at weekends breakfast is served until 2pm. Takeaways are available if you'd rather picnic in the park.

benugo.com
Lincoln's Inn Fields, WC2A 3LJ
Holborn tube

Mingle at Marylebone Farmers' Market
Introduce your dog to a world of new smells

——

You meet a classy breed of dog in Marylebone, and the crowd here is no exception. As at most farmers' markets, the atmosphere is friendly and everyone – customers and stallholders – seems very pro-dog. And where else can you browse food and drink with your companion by your side? The 30 or so stalls here include Honeypie Bakery, Longshore Fish (all the way from Blakeney in Norfolk), Moreton Mushrooms and The Parsons Nose (try their sausage and onions in a bun). The market runs on Sundays, from 10am until 2pm. Take cash!

lfm.org.uk
Cramer Street car park, W1U 4EW
Baker Street tube

Lincoln's Inn Fields

Outsider Tart

WEST LONDON

The living is easy for the pampered pets of west London. There are classy shops, groomers and walkers on tap, and lots of well-tended grass to run around on. The cafés and restaurants here are inclined to look kindly on four-legged customers too. If you're visiting the area, this ease makes for a great day out – just don't expect any hill walks, or much in the way of wilderness.

Get your feet wet along Hammersmith riverside

River views and historic, hound-friendly pubs

———

Every pub along this route is pro-dog, and all have enticing outdoor spaces, so your only decision will be choosing where to stop. Starting from Hammersmith tube, head to Hammersmith Bridge and drop down to the riverside. Almost immediately, you come to the Blue Anchor and the Rutland (a rare Taylor Walker pub in Fuller's Brewery territory). Then there's a chance of some green space, as you pass Furnival Gardens, before arriving at the atmospheric Dove (owned by Fuller's since 1796) – they love dogs here, but if your mutt is large it may all feel a bit cramped. The next tavern on the walk is the Old Ship, which is blessed with two terraces and an adjacent lawn. A little further along is the Black Lion, set back from the river, but with a large beer garden and an indoor skittle alley. Continue along Hammersmith Terrace to scenic Chiswick Mall, where the houses are on one side of the road and the gardens on the other, next to the river. Here, the road regularly floods (the houses all have flood defences) – if it's clear, continue to the end, before retracing your steps back to Hammersmith and those alluring hostelries.

Lower Mall, W6 to Chiswick Mall, W4
Hammersmith tube

Hammersmith riverside

Outsider Tart

Tuck in at Outsider Tart
A barkery/bakery in Chiswick

⸺

You and Fido can both eat baked goods at this American-style café and bakery, as a selection of home-made dog treats are always available in a retro dispenser. The café serves US cakes, comfort food (chilli is a favourite) and brunches, and accommodates dogs of all sizes. A range of dog biscuits can be ordered online – among the flavours are chicken and cheese, and peanut butter.

outsidertart.com
83 Chiswick High Road, W4 2EF
Turnham Green tube

Delight in Chiswick House Gardens
Not just any old walk in the park

⸺

These restored eighteenth-century gardens make for a classy walk, with formal avenues, sweet-smelling shrubbery, architectural features, a lake and sloping lawns. Dogs will relish the chance to snuffle around in the woodland area to the south and west of the property. Areas where dogs aren't allowed (the walled kitchen gardens) or should be on a lead are clearly marked; the grounds are beautifully maintained and there are plenty of waste bins. The café restricts hounds to the covered terrace, where dog bowls are dotted around. Don't miss the annual Chiswick House Dog Show in September – there are lots of stalls, and classes including Naughtiest Dog.

chgt.org.uk
Chiswick House Gardens, W4 2RP
Turnham Green tube or Chiswick rail

Chiswick House Gardens

Become a regular at the Scarsdale Tavern

Head for a pint after a stroll in Holland Park

———

When the dog's water is brought to the table before the wine, you know the waitress's heart is in the right place. The Scarsdale is set on one of the loveliest squares in a swanky area, but is a surprisingly unpretentious pub (Fuller's). Yes, there's an ambitious menu and a display of champagne bottles, but there's also a TV showing sport and a bunch of regulars. Dogs can settle in the small, very green beer garden at the front, the dining area with open kitchen at the back, or the sociable bar room.

scarsdaletavern.co.uk
23A Edwardes Square, W8 6HE
High Street Kensington tube or
Kensington (Olympia) rail

Go crazy at Mutz Nutz

The one-stop shop for Notting Hill hounds

———

The memorably named Mutz Nutz is a small pet shop that packs a lot in: you can buy everything from natural treats and smart Hunter drinking bowls to diamanté collars and pink tennis balls. Or treat your puppy to a Snuggle 'pet companion'. WildWash grooming products are another line – and they're used in the spa. Doggy day care is also offered.

themutznutz.com
221 Westbourne Park Road, W11 1EA
Westbourne Park tube

TOP TEN
Dog-friendly hotels

Ace Hotel, *Shoreditch*
Not only can they stay at
this trendy hotel, but pets
have the run of the place
(apart from the restaurant).
acehotel.com

**Aloft London ExCeL,
*Docklands***
There's no surcharge for
beds and treats at this
international chain; what's
more, they accept dogs
weighing up to 18kg.
aloftlondonexcel.com

Bermondsey Square Hotel,
Bermondsey
Dog beds and treats are
provided at this modern
hotel, which is handily
placed for dog-tastic
Bermondsey Street.
bermondseysquarehotel.co.uk

**Ibis Southwark Rose,
*Borough***
Not every hotel in this chain
accepts dogs, but this one
does and is a reasonably priced
option close to the centre.
ibis.com

**The Milestone Hotel,
*Kensington***
Luxury boutique hotel opposite
Kensington Gardens, where
the welcome includes a hamper
just for your dog, and there's
a long list of doggy services.
milestonehotel.com

**The Portobello Hotel,
*Notting Hill***
You have to bring your own
bowls, beds and so on to
this laid-back townhouse
hotel, but the vibe is a very
welcoming one.
portobellohotel.com

Rosewood, *Holborn*
Pearl the golden retriever fronts
up the enticing pet package on
this swanky hotel's website.
Lincoln's Inn Fields is the
nearest place for a run-around.
rosewoodhotels.com

Russell's, *Hackney*
A modish and affordable B&B
that welcomes dogs; say hello
to resident whippet Reggie.
russellsofclapton.com

**St Pancras Renaissance,
*King's Cross***
The ultimate in deluxe railway
hotels accepts small to medium
dogs (up to 10kg).
marriott.co.uk

South Place Hotel, *City*
Small- to medium-sized pets are
welcomed at this stylish hotel,
part of the D&D restaurant
group. Expect beds, bowls and
a welcome treat.
southplacehotel.com

Make a purchase at Pedlars
Feel at home with this dog-loving store

——

Pedlars sells stylish, retro-inspired gifts and homewares, including dog-themed goodies such as framed posters and ceramic bowls. There's a comfortable café at the back of the store, plus a few pavement tables – hounds get an access-all-areas pass. Settle back on one of the big squishy cushions with an Allpress coffee and avocado on rye, and enter your faithful companion into the Dog of the Week competition (see the website for details – and a photo gallery of winners).

pedlars.co.uk
128 Talbot Road, W11 1JA
Ladbroke Grove tube

Enjoy the manicured acres of Holland Park
Join the lapdogs getting their daily exercise

——

Stretching from Holland Park Avenue down to High Street Kensington, Holland Park packs a lot into its 55 acres. Of most interest to dogs are the wilder woodland areas to the north, and the grassy open spaces. It's a sociable dog-walking spot, best suited to small- or medium-sized pooches who are happy to be on a lead. The café is dog-friendly, or you could just nab a bench and watch the pampered local pooches go by.

rbkc.gov.uk
Illchester Place, W8 6LU
High Street Kensington or Holland Park tube

Cultivate a love of plants at Clifton Nurseries
Bucolic garden centre with a charming café

———

Let your dog stop and smell the roses at this Maida Vale nursery. Wander through rows of fruit and olive trees, bedding plants, grasses and climbers, and all manner of flowers. There are sections devoted to pots and containers, and several handsome greenhouses variously holding indoor plants, garden furniture and accessories (seeds, tools, candles and cards). In addition, a 'farm shop' sells deli items, plus dog treats from Pooch & Mutt and floral collars from Blossom Co. The Quince Tree café is in yet another charming greenhouse, and serves a mix of brunch/lunch dishes (soup of the day, big salads, beef burger with fries) and tea and cake. Your four-legged friend is welcome everywhere.

clifton.co.uk
5A Clifton Villas, W9 2PH
Warwick Avenue tube

Stock up at Animal Fair
A one-stop shop in Kensington

———

Animal Fair claims to be the largest pet store in central London, and having seen the Abingdon Road shop crammed with stock, it's hard to disagree. Whatever your dog requires, from beds to ball throwers, you'll find it here. The atmosphere is reassuringly sensible, and staff are happy (and qualified) to offer advice. There's also a grooming parlour, and boarding (in the countryside) can be arranged.

animal-fair.co.uk
17 Abingdon Road, W8 6AH
High Street Kensington tube

TOP TEN
Lapdog haunts

Andrew Edmunds, *Soho*
A Soho stalwart with a fine wine list. They might even take larger pooches if you ask nicely, though space is limited.
andrewedmunds.com

Bellanger, *Islington*
An Alsatian-inspired (the area, not the dog), all-day brasserie, serving everything from cocktails to three-course meals. Your lapdog will love it.
bellanger.co.uk

Bibendum Oyster Bar, *South Kensington*
Eat seafood in style, with your shih-tzu in attendance, at this iconic hangout.
bibendum.co.uk

Daphne's, *South Kensington*
The pretty conservatory at this classic ladies-who-lunch haunt allows dogs at lunchtime.
daphnes-restaurant.co.uk

Dock Kitchen, *Ladbroke Grove*
Industrial-looking canal-side dining room, with a modern menu and a fondness for dogs.
dockkitchen.co.uk

La Fromagerie, *Marylebone*
Small, well-behaved dogs can sniff the air appreciatively in this cheese specialist and deli. There are café tables dotted throughout.
lafromagerie.co.uk

Gastro, *Clapham*
Casual French bistro with a doggy entente cordiale.

Megan's, *Fulham*
Café and grill, with a soft spot for four-legged diners.
megans.co.uk

The Orchard, *Brockley*
They're so accommodating at this independent neighbourhood brasserie that a St Bernard would probably be considered.
thebrockleyorchard.com

Polpo, *across London*
Venetian small-plates specialist with a warm welcome for lapdogs and their owners.
polpo.co.uk

Hampstead Heath

NORTH WEST LONDON

In dog world, north west London means one thing: Hampstead Heath. Owners willingly travel miles to enjoy the carefully maintained space, and it's a lucky hound that lives nearby. A happy side effect of the Heath's dominance is that most cafés and pubs within striking distance open their doors to muddy mutts; here, we've highlighted some of the most notable ones.

Be thankful for Hampstead Heath
Dog nirvana in NW3

A glorious open space, so large (790 acres) you can happily get lost in it, going wherever your dog's nose takes you. Foxes, squirrels, rabbits and lots of smaller creatures are all to be found here. There is woodland, with plenty of fallen trees for truffling around; wild undergrowth as well as grassy stretches; and lots of hills to gambol on. Hounds can be off the lead in many sections of the Heath, without a road in sight. There's water in the form of ponds, too, but be aware of birdlife, and stay well away from the bathing ponds.

The Brew House café at Kenwood House has water bowls, but dogs must stay outside; the same is true of Parliament Hill café (near the tennis courts at the Highgate Road entrance). It's easy to find indoor refreshments nearby though; dog-friendly pubs and cafés ring Hampstead Heath.

cityoflondon.gov.uk
Hampstead Heath, NW3
Hampstead tube, Gospel Oak or
Hampstead Heath rail

Hampstead Heath

MY DOG

Henrietta Morrison

With the number of parks and outdoor spaces available, London is a brilliant place for dogs to hang out. Lily is mainly to be found in Hampstead as she lives (and works) there. Hampstead Heath is nirvana for dogs – no leads required in the vast majority of places to roam about.

There are also plenty of wide open spaces to play ball or frisbee together, as well as ponds your dog can swim in – the Vale of Health Pond being one of the most popular. Kenwood House has a great outdoor café serving delicious food for humans with lots of bowls of water scattered around. The Wells Pub is another super spot for lunch or dinner – they even have a doggy menu, so you can order a bowl of food for your dog and not feel guilty whilst you are tucking into your filet steak.

Hampstead is an incredibly friendly place for dogs; most shops will allow you to bring your dog in and some even have a bowl of water outside, such as the Hampstead Butcher on Rosslyn Hill. If your dog is feeling peckish whilst out for a walk, then you can drop into the Mutt Hut located at the Lido entrance to the Heath – they have stacks of snacks including Lily's own snack bars.

Make merry at the Bull & Last
Perfect for a post-Heath feast

——

For a slap-up lunch after a walk on the
Heath, it has to be the Bull & Last. Dogs
are restricted to the ground-floor bar area –
but as this convivial room is the heart of the
pub, that's not really a hardship. There are
pavement tables out front too. On Sundays,
the restaurant-standard menu is supplemented
by big roasts. It's such a meaty pub that dogs
may be in line for a treat. You can still just
pop in for a pint though – a good range of
microbreweries are represented.

thebullandlast.co.uk
168 Highgate Road, NW5 1QS
Gospel Oak rail

Make a beeline for the Southampton Arms
A gem of a pub in Gospel Oak

——

A walk on the Heath followed by a beer
and a pork pie at the Southampton Arms is
something of a tradition in NW5. Especially
on Sunday lunchtimes, when the place is full
of dogs hoping for a morsel of pie or the mighty
roast pork bap. Proudly independent, the pub
sells beers and ciders from small, equally
independent breweries and operates a simple
(but effective) food offering. The dark woody
interior is snug and has a clean dog bowl by
the entrance; there's a congenial beer garden at
the back. What's more, staff play great music.

thesouthamptonarms.co.uk
139 Highgate Road, NW5 1LE
Gospel Oak rail

The Southampton Arms

TOP TEN

Gifts for dog lovers (put a dog on it)

choccywoccydoodah.com
If you know someone who
loves chocolate and dogs,
Choccywoccydoodah's
Westie puppy is made out
of solid white chocolate
and weighs 1kg.

creatureclothes.com
Match your belt or wrist
cuff to the dog's collar, or
buy a bone-shaped key ring
– just some of the gifts
available alongside the
UK-made dog gear.

houndworthy.com
Website with a charming
selection of dog-themed
vintage jewellery, modern
prints, stylish T-shirts and
dog bags. It sells lovely
dog gear too.

growler-london.co.uk
A gorgeous online collection
spanning vintage dog figurines
and modish T-shirts.

londonpooch.co.uk
Illustrator Joy FitzSimmons
sells a range of adorable
dachshund-themed cards,
prints and gifts (tea towels,
notebooks, shopping bags).

lovemydog.co.uk
Invest in a chic pet carrier
from this London-based
designer – they're made from
Scottish tweed with Italian
leather straps.

**Pets in Portraits,
National Portrait Gallery**
An updated edition of a
collection of portraits of
well-known people and their
animals. Dogs feature heavily.

**Pub Dogs of London,
Freight Books**
London photographer
Fiona Freund has taken
portraits of dogs in pubs;
poet Graham Fulton has
added some words.

sunofwolves.com
Striking mugs ('In dog
we trust'), totes, flags and
more, from a couple of
young designers inspired
by their dog Wolf.

**Woolly Woofers Knitting
Pattern Book, Quadrille**
For dog-lovers who knit
– over 20 designs by
knitwear star and dog
owner Debbie Bliss.

Spruce up at the Mutt Hut
Muddy dogs a speciality

Owned by a local couple, the Mutt Hutt is a dog-grooming business, handily placed on the edge of the Heath (near the Parliament Hill Lido entrance). The green hut is easy to spot, emblazoned as it is with the motto 'because they're woof it'. As well as grooming services, treats and accessories are also sold, and they offer free poo bags and water to rinse off muddy dogs coming off the Heath.

the-mutt-hut.co.uk
Gordon House Road, NW5 1LT
Gospel Oak rail

The Spaniards Inn

Go back in time in Golders Hill Park
Escape the hurly-burly in NW11

——

If the thought of rough and tumble on the Heath is just too much for your nervous pooch, or you have a dog who can't be trusted outside a fenced-in area, then Golders Hill Park is the answer. Dogs have to be kept on leads in this well-maintained formal park, which boasts lots of lovely lawns, flower displays and a duck pond. For refreshments, try the Old Bull & Bush, just opposite the main entrance to the park.

cityoflondon.gov.uk
West Heath Avenue, NW11 7QP
Golders Green or Hampstead tube

Cosy up to the fire at the Spaniards Inn
One of London's oldest pubs, on the edge of Hampstead Heath

——

The wood-panelled Spaniards is a snug place to be in the winter months, when dogs and walkers can dry out in front of the fire. On sunny days, the large beer garden (set back from the road) comes into its own. Whatever the weather, on Sundays the pub is busy with families tucking into roast lunches, accompanied by dogs on the scrounge.

thespaniardshampstead.co.uk
Spaniards Road, NW3 7JJ
210 bus, or Golders Green or Hampstead tube

Gaucho Hampstead

Get dressed up for Doggy Sunday
Eat in style at Gaucho Hampstead

The NW3 branch of the Argentinian steak house literally rolls out the red carpet for pooches on Doggy Sundays. Once inside, they get the run of the restaurant on this once-a-month treat; tables are cleared on the outside terrace to make a play area – complete with seesaw. Bacon treats and mini empanadas keep hunger at bay. For doting humans, there's a Sunday roast (available all day), alongside the regular steak options.

gauchorestaurants.com
64 Heath Street, NW3 1DN
Hampstead tube

TOP TEN
Good causes

All Dogs Matter
A rescue and rehoming
charity in north London,
with a big network of foster
carers looking after the
dogs until they can be
placed with new owners.
alldogsmatter.co.uk

Battersea Dogs & Cats Home
The daddy of them all
(est. 1860), Battersea
looks after more than
8,000 animals a year.
battersea.org.uk

Blue Cross
Pet care for people who
can't afford veterinary fees.
Blue Cross have centres
and mobile clinics
across London.
bluecross.org.uk

Dogs Trust
Rehoming dogs across
21 centres, the Dogs Trust
also offers support to dog
owners who are homeless.
dogstrust.org.uk

Guide Dogs
Help can be given in many
ways, from donations to
volunteering or rehoming
a 'failed' guide dog.
guidedogs.org.uk

The Mayhew Animal Home
Based in Kensal Rise, but
operating around the world,
the Mayhew looks after dogs
but also runs programmes
such as TheraPaws – dogs
who visit care homes.
themayhew.org

Oldies Club
As the name suggests, the
charity rehomes and fosters
older dogs.
oldies.org.uk

PDSA
The People's Dispensary
for Sick Animals is a charity
that provides free support
for people in need, and
promotes pet health.
pdsa.org.uk

Pets as Therapy
Pets can be trained to
volunteer in many ways –
from encouraging rehab in
stroke patients to helping
children to gain confidence
in reading aloud.
petsastherapy.org

RSPCA
The best-known animal
welfare charity, and star
of Channel 5's The Dog
Rescuers. The RSPCA rescues,
rehabilitates and campaigns.
rspca.org.uk

Hair of the Dog

NORTH LONDON

There are some great, traffic-free walks to be had in north London –
as well as the obvious parks, there are linear walks along canals
and disused railway lines. It's also an area blessed with convivial
pubs and an above-average number of attractive beer gardens,
which makes places such as Highgate, Islington or Primrose Hill
top destinations for a Sunday excursion.

Bask in the beer gardens at the Red Lion & Sun

A pretty gastropub well placed for walks

———

Highgate has no shortage of drinking establishments, all of them dog-friendly and many of them with beer gardens (the one at the Flask is particularly appealing), but gastropub the Red Lion & Sun wins our vote. Not only is the food good, but there are charming beer gardens to the front and the rear of the pub. Staff are friendly, and have created an easy-going vibe: you could come here for Sunday lunch and stay all afternoon. We've spotted everything from a giant white poodle to a King Charles spaniel under the tables here. If the pub is full, the Bull just up the road has dog biscuits and a nice outdoor space.

theredlionandsun.com
25 North Road, N6 4BE
Highgate tube

Dine with four-legged friends at Market

A Camden bolthole for you and your dog

———

So relaxed is the dog policy here that you can just turn up with Fido (though it's always polite to ask first). Step off traffic-heavy Parkway into this calm, pared-down modern British restaurant, for dishes such as lemon sole with brown shrimp and samphire, followed by strawberry and custard Eton mess or Neal's Yard cheeses with crackers and chutney. There's a great-value set lunch during the week, and a terrific brunch menu at weekends, featuring everything from buttermilk pancakes with berries to a slap-up roast.

marketrestaurant.co.uk
43 Parkway, NW1 7PN
Camden Town tube

The Red Lion & Sun

Battersea Dogs & Cats Home Annual Reunion & Fun Day, *September*
This fundraiser is open to all (not just ex-Battersea pets) and features displays, stalls and the odd celeb. Held in Battersea Park.

Bermondsey Street Festival Dog Show, *September*
Enter a pooch for the dog show, or just go along for the good doggy vibes.

Bring Your Dog to Work Day, *June*
A nationwide fundraiser for All Dogs Matter, the rescue and rehoming charity.

Brockwell Park Dog Show, *July*
One of the best-loved events in the south London canine calendar. Every year there's a different theme, and competitions include Dogs Got Talent.

Chiswick House Dog Show, *September*
West London's well-organised show has all kinds of classes to enter, from naughtiest to best rescue – in the gorgeous setting of Chiswick House grounds.

Discover Dogs, *October*
The big one – meet all kinds of breeds, watch the competitions, chat to owners. Held at ExCeL. One drawback – you can't take your dog.

The Great British Dog Walk, *Spring*
Held in National Trust properties – including Osterley Park, west London – to raise money for Hearing Dogs for Deaf People.

Muddy Dog Challenge, *Spring*
You and your dog can take part in 2.5km and 5km obstacle courses and raise money for Battersea Dogs Home. London's 2016 challenge was held in Brockwell Park.

Pup Aid, *September*
An anti-puppy-farming jamboree on Primrose Hill, held to raise awareness but with lots of fun (stalls, competitions, food) along the way. There's a high celebrity supporter count.

RSPCA BIG Walkies, *year-round*
Fundraising walks all over the country, with plenty of events in or just outside London. If you don't have your own dog, you can volunteer to help.

Meet at the Marquess Tavern
Enjoy a Sunday get-together in style

———

A big, handsome pub that rolls out the welcome mat for dogs. There's water and biscuits by the front door, and dog-centric scatter cushions ('reserved for the dog') everywhere. Decor is quirky but comfortable throughout, but the brightly decorated beer garden, softened by tubs of bamboo plants, is the place to be on sunny days. Drinks include a small range of cocktails. Thought has gone into the food too: there are sausage rolls and Scotch eggs on the bar, and more substantial offerings such as pulled pork in a brioche bun with fries and slaw. If exercise is needed, the pub is opposite one of the entrances for the New River Walk.

themarquessn1.co.uk
32 Canonbury Street, N1 2TB
Highbury & Islington tube or rail, or
Essex Road rail

The Marquess Tavern

Take the towpath from Islington to Hackney

Get close to canal life on this 1.5-mile amble

———

Islington doesn't have much in the way of green space, so this stretch of towpath is a big plus. Just remember that speeding cyclists are a menace to dogs and pedestrians before 10am and after 4pm, so time your walk accordingly to avoid spooking your pooch. The Narrowboat pub (on the canal at St Peter's Street, at the Islington end), the Towpath Cafe and the Barge House (next to each other on the canal near De Beauvoir Crescent) and Poco (above the canal on Pritchard's Road, near Broadway Market) are all good, dog-friendly refreshment stops. Slightly further afield, at the Islington end, head for the Charles Lamb or the Duke of Cambridge; in the other direction, there's always Broadway Market.

N1 to E2
Angel tube or London Fields rail

Towpath Café

Canal towpath

New River Walk

Trace the New River Walk
Get from Canonbury to Islington Green without traffic
——

A welcome thread of green running through Islington, the New River Walk allows you to meander from Canonbury down towards the southern end of Essex Road without encountering much traffic. There are little parks, children's play areas and some impressive trees along the way, not to mention lots of wildlife, particularly ducks and moorhens. Being a very urban walk, it's also easy to leave the path for a coffee (the Place, on Canonbury Place, has water for dogs and coffee for humans) or something stronger (the Myddleton Arms, the Marquess Tavern and the Canonbury Tavern all have beer gardens).

islington.gov.uk
N1
Canonbury rail

Go traffic-free on the Parkland Walk
Retrace the path of an old railway line
——

Joggers are the only real hazard on this stretch of defunct railway line – otherwise, it's a very peaceful, leafy stroll. There's the occasional reminder of past glories (the remains of a platform, for instance), plus a small skateboard ramp and some graffiti, but mainly the path is green, and blissfully traffic-free. The south section of the walk (1.7 miles) runs from the edge of Finsbury Park to Highgate tube; you can then wander through Queen's Wood and Highgate Wood before joining the much shorter northern section (750m from the edge of Highgate Wood to Muswell Hill). For refreshments, you'll have to rely on the parks at either end (the Pavilion Café in Highgate Wood is nicest, with a designated outdoor dog area, but beware long queues at weekends), or venture into Highgate where there are many dog-friendly pubs.

N4 to N10
Finsbury Park tube or rail and Highgate tube

Parkland Walk

TOP TEN

More parks – inner London

Burgess Park, *SE5*
One of London's newer parks (created in the 1950s), the largest park in Southwark (140 acres) is a welcome green space in a busy area.

Dulwich Park, *SE21*
A well-kept park with a bit of everything (lake, wildflower meadow, old trees), including a dog walk around the perimeter.

Finsbury Park, *N4*
Classic Victorian park, with plenty of room to run around in. It's also the start of the Parkland Walk.

Highbury Fields, *N5*
Though it's only 29 acres, this is the biggest green space in Islington and a magnet for the local dog community.

Hilly Fields, *SE4*
Much-loved local park, with lots of grassy open spaces, uphill walking and amazing views towards central London.

Mile End Park, *E3*
Modern, linear park with lovely landscaping and direct access to Regent's Canal. There's an annual dog show too.

Ravenscourt Park, *W6*
A well-used local park with good facilities and a lovely big grassy area for dogs to romp in.

Ruskin Park, *SE5*
An Edwardian park with a great variety of trees on its 36 acres, and very popular with dog walkers.

Tooting Common, *SW17*
Grassland, woods and ponds, plus seasonal treats such as bluebells, with plenty of room to roam.

Wormwood Scrubs, *W12*
The 200 acres of mostly open grassland is a favourite with dogs who need a lot of exercise.

Explore the area around Granary Square

A new area of London to investigate

———

The development behind King's Cross station has produced something of an urban playground, with outdoor screenings, street food markets and art installations adding life to a thoroughly modern part of town. Dogs will like the canal walk, the new green spaces (such as neat Lewis Cubitt Park) and the chance to mess about in the Granary Square fountains. There are lots of places to rest your legs – try the AstroTurf-covered steps down to the canal – and plenty of cafés with outdoor seating. Modern pub the Lighterman is happy to host dogs in the airy ground-floor bar.

kingscross.co.uk
N1C
King's Cross St Pancras tube

Stroll along Regent's Park Road

A dog-friendly street with a park attached

———

With Primrose Hill at the end of the road for views and exercise, and a number of welcoming cafés and bars in the neighbourhood, tree-lined Regent's Park Road is an upmarket dog's delight. It's a well-appointed stretch of swanky boutiques (many of them happy to see you and your pooch) and cafés (many of them with tables and dog bowls outside). Try Greenberry Café, where every size of hound is welcome, and the menu mutates from egg and avocado brunches to bistro suppers. Close by are foodie pubs the Lansdowne and the Engineer. What's more, at no.132 there's the long-established Primrose Hill Pets, a trad pet shop which also offers grooming.

NW1
Chalk Farm tube

The Albion

Make a special trip to Barkers
A one-stop shop in Muswell Hill
—

This is one impressive dog store. It's spacious, with plenty of room for everything from foodstuffs (packaged and frozen) to flea and worm treatments. Stock is temptingly displayed: you can come in for a collar and leave with a cupcake from the Barking Bakery or a mat inscribed 'wipe paws and carry on'. Sample puzzles and chews are left out for dogs to try. There's a modern spa and grooming room at the back (clearly visible through glass) and they also offer microchipping. Staff are helpful and know their stuff. Barkers also hosts get-togethers – on our visit, a Silly Sausage Dachshund Social was being advertised.

barkersfordogs.com
70 Fortis Green Road, N10 3HN
Bus 134, East Finchley tube of Highgate tube

Visit the Albion, a country pub in N1
A beer garden made for lazy weekends
—

Though the pub interior is nice and cosy, with plenty of squishy sofas and log fires, the splendid beer garden is the Albion's not-so-secret weapon. It's big, but it's also charming, with plenty of greenery, tumbling wisteria and a kitchen garden along one edge. A dog and his owner could happily stretch out here for the afternoon. Well-executed gastro-pub classics include giant portions of fish and triple-cooked chips and a good-looking cheeseboard, and wine is more of a feature here than in many pubs.

the-albion.co.uk
10 Thornhill Road, N1 1HW
Highbury & Islington tube or rail,
or Caledonian Road & Barnsbury rail

Discover Hair of the Dog in Highgate

A stylish pet store and grooming parlour

—

Described by the owners as a dog and cat boutique, Hair of the Dog has an arresting window display and an array of leads and harnesses, accessories and foodstuffs. Inside are smart designer collars, toys and gift books, and a big selection of packaged foods, from Lily's Kitchen meals to Pooch's dog treats. Grooming is a big deal too: there are grooming products and, at the rear, the grooming parlour, complete with a lovely little courtyard space.

hairofthedoglondon.com
24 Highgate High Street, N6 5JG
Highgate tube

Try the Park Theatre Café Bar

An oasis behind Finsbury Park station

—

Buzzing with theatre-going crowds in the evening, the café is equally popular as a community hangout at other times. It's open all day, starting with breakfasts and running through sausage rolls and sandwiches to supper platters (meze, cheese and charcuterie boards). There's a water bowl at the ready for dogs; Union coffee, Teapigs tea and a cocktail happy hour keep humans happy. Handy for Finsbury Park and the Parkland Walk, and with a concrete interior that a bit of mud can't harm.

parktheatre.co.uk
Clifton Terrace, N4 3JP
Finsbury Park tube or rail

Hair of the Dog

Epping Forest

NORTH EAST LONDON

Green spaces abound in what is considered a very built-up area, with Hackney Marshes, Clissold Park and Epping Forest topping a list that also includes small pleasures such as Abney Park Cemetery. By way of contrast, this is also where you'll find some of London's hippest hounds – Hackney's Broadway Market and Chatsworth Road scenes are very dog-friendly, whether or not your mutt qualifies as a fashion accessory.

Walk the waterways of north east London
Stretch those canine legs

——

The Hackney Wick to Tottenham Hale section of the Lea Valley Walk is a great way to introduce some variety into your dog's life – while never straying far from a refreshment stop. You could start in the beautifully landscaped Queen Elizabeth Olympic Park, or head straight for the towpath, direction north. If wide open spaces are required, Hackney Marshes is an easy detour east; this segues into Walthamstow Marshes. At Lea Bridge Weir, the popular Princess of Wales has liquid refreshment for man and beast, and tables overlooking the water. A little further along, on the west side of the River Lea, there's the pretty Springfield Park, with the handily placed Riverside Café offering fry-ups or tea and cake, as well as a dog bowl. Parts of the walk are unexpectedly bucolic: you might see horses from the Lee Valley Riding Centre; you'll certainly see plenty of birdlife; and there are times when you can't see any dwellings other than canal boats. Much less crowded than the Regent's Canal, and a whole new set of smells for the hound.

tfl.gov.uk/modes/walking/lea-valley
E9 to N17
Hackney Wick and Tottenham Hale tube or rail

River Lea canal

Hackney Marshes

Lizzy's

Mix with Stoke Newington dogs at Lizzy's
A park café that's worth a detour

A small kiosk/café with a strong sense of community, where the warm welcome very much includes dogs (check out the dogs' gallery on the website). What's more, the food is a cut above most park café offerings. You can get a bacon roll or a fish-finger sarnie, but there's also a BLT or smoked cream corn with soft boiled egg and jalapeño on sourdough or rye toast. Flat white and espresso are served alongside tea and home-made cake. All the seating is open air; there are deckchairs when it's warm, heaters for when it's cold, and fresh flowers on every table. The view is of the garden-like square, transformed by Islington Council in 2005 from a grotty traffic island to a popular mini-park.

lizzysonthegreen.com
Newington Green roundabout, N16 9PX
Canonbury rail

Epping Forest
London's largest open space

—

The walk possibilities are seemingly endless here, as you'd expect with over 6,000 acres to play with. It's a mix of woodland, heathland and grassland, with lots of lakes and ponds, plus four visitor centres. There are nine marked trails, useful for newbies; these range from 45-minute strolls (Gifford Wood Trail) to 3-hour hikes (Oak Trail). High Beach is a good starting point if you've never been before – there's a visitor centre (with loos) and tea huts. Watch out for mountain bikes and horses along the way.

cityoflondon.gov.uk
E4 and IG10
Theydon Bois tube, or Chingford rail

See and be seen at Broadway Market
Soak up the social scene in Hackney

—

Saturdays are when hipster dogs come to sniff each other out at Broadway Market. There's much posing amid the food, clothes and craft stalls (there are yet more pitches in Netil Market round the corner) and most of the cafés have pavement tables so you can watch the world go by. L'eau à La Bouche, a French deli/café serving coffee and snacks (and bacon ends for very lucky dogs), is a favourite hangout. Other top picks are the Cat & Mutton pub and eco-friendly Poco (on the canal bridge), which does a great brunch.

broadwaymarket.co.uk
E8 4QJ
Cambridge Heath or London Fields rail

Take a quiet stroll in Abney Park Cemetery
Soak up the atmosphere in Stoke Newington

—

Stokey dogs are lucky to have both Clissold Park and Abney Park Cemetery on their doorstep. The cemetery is the place to head for a quiet, less sociable mooch, and it's cool on hot days. Dogs have trees, fungi and animals to investigate – there's lots of dense undergrowth to snuffle through – while the memorials provide humans with food for thought. Abney Park is one of the 'Magnificent Seven' Victorian cemeteries, and is equally lovely in winter or summer.

hackney.gov.uk
Stoke Newington High Street, N16 0LH
Stoke Newington rail

Spend a few hours at the Bell
A hit with Walthamstow waggers

—

Dogs compete with babies in this congenial boozer. The Bell serves great grub (share the mighty hog board) and always has an excellent selection of ales on tap. The paved terrace at the back of the pub is a small but glorious suntrap – always home to a sunbathing dog or two. You can easily forget that you're on noisy Forest Road and were supposed to be elsewhere two hours ago. In winter, your pooch can curl up by the fire while you take on the tasty Sunday roast, another Bell staple.

belle17.com
617 Forest Road, E17 4NE
Walthamstow Central tube or rail

Animals in War, *W2*
A bronze dog joins a horse and two pack mules in this 2004 memorial, paid for by public donations and designed by David Backhouse. Find it where Upper Brook Street crosses Park Lane.

Blind Beggar & his Dog, *E2*
Sited within the Cranbrook Estate in Bethnal Green, this elegant 1957 statue by Elizabeth Frink can be seen from Roman Road.

Brown Dog, *SW8*
This charming replacement for the infamous anti-vivisection dog (removed in 1910) is by Nicola Hicks. It can be found near the Old English Garden in Battersea Park.

Byron, *W1*
The poet with his Newfoundland Boatswain, by R.C. Belt. You'll have to view from a distance, as it's stranded in the middle of Park Lane (at the Hyde Park Corner end).

Dog & Pot, *SE1*
A sculpture by Mike Painter, inspired by Charles Dickens' description of a shop sign. It was erected on Blackfriars Road (on the corner of Union Street) in 2013 to celebrate the bicentenary of his birth.

Queen Mother, *SW1*
Naturally, corgis are featured in this memorial to the Queen Mother. Spot them on one of the friezes behind her statue on the Mall.

Richard Green, *E14*
The local ship-owner and philanthropist, with his Newfoundland dog Hector. The statue (1886) is by Edward Wyon, and is on East India Dock Road, outside Poplar Baths.

Sir Robert Grosvenor, *SW1*
The first Marquess of Westminster has two hunting dogs at his feet in this 1998 statue in Belgrave Square; it's by Jonathan Wylder.

Thomas Sayers, *N6*
A life-size sculpture of Lion, Thomas Sayers' dog, guards his monument in Highgate West Cemetery. Sayers was a famous Victorian bare-knuckle boxer.

William Hogarth, *W4*
The statue of the painter and his dog Trump is by Jim Mathieson and was unveiled in 2001. It stands on Chiswick High Road.

Pack and Clowder

Pop into Pack and Clowder
Chatsworth Road's very own dog shop

A charming shop, where you can get all sorts of carefully sourced goodies for dogs (and, whisper it, cats). Foodstuffs, all without additives or preservatives, range from a jar of sweet potato chews to freezers full of raw food; the latter is very popular, with around 100kg a week sold. There are pre-packaged lines from Billy + Margot, Zealandia and Lily's Kitchen. The rest of the stock runs from tartan bow ties and dog toys to collapsible drinking bowls and British-made beds. Owner Jackie is happy to advise on anything from dog food to local hangouts; she also offers grooming.

packandclowder.co.uk
18 Chatsworth Road, E5 0LP
Homerton rail

Make friends in Clissold Park
A very Stoke Newington type of space

—

Hang out in Chatsworth Road
Shop, eat and meet the E5 locals

—

A much-loved community hub, Clissold Park is the go-to green space for sociable dogs. Those needing a bit more personal space would be better off elsewhere, but for friends and variety, not to mention a café, Clissold Park wins out. There are places in the park where dogs should be on a lead, and some areas (the animal enclosure, the children's playground) where they're not allowed at all – these are clearly marked. The café in the Grade II-listed Clissold House looks grander than it is, but it's a good spot for a coffee; dogs are only allowed on the large terrace. Walk your hound here and you'll be part of a dog group in no time.

hackney.gov.uk
Green Lanes, N16 9HJ
Manor House tube or Stoke Newington rail

A friendly street, with lots of independent businesses, where dogs are welcome in most cafés, restaurants and non-food shops. At Cooper & Wolf staff may even break off from serving Swedish meatballs and cinnamon buns to admire particularly cute specimens; naturally, they have a dog bowl. Dorée and Venetia's are other good stops for coffee and a snack; the Elderfield pub, round the corner on Elderfield Road, welcomes all comers too. Don't miss Pack and Clowder pet shop either. The street even has a dog show (as part of the annual Chatsworth Road Festival in September). The popular Sunday market is a great opportunity for parading your pooch, as is Rushmore Sunday Market, an off-shoot in Rushmore Primary School yard. Millfields Park is handily placed at the northern end of the road.

chatsworthroade5.co.uk
E5
Clapton or Homerton rail

Let the dogs out in Lloyd Park
A popular place for walkies in Walthamstow

—

Hunt down the Clapton Hart
Find a cosy corner in this big old boozer

—

Picturesque Lloyd Park has two large fields (one in which dogs are allowed to roam free), a small enclosed off-lead area (converted from an old grassy playground), and is also home to the beautifully landscaped gardens of the William Morris Gallery, full of plants that appear in Morris's designs. Developments in recent years have boosted Lloyd Park's profile – it has a range of great facilities and a dog-friendly, decent café, Le Délice in the Park. The now annual Walthamstow Garden Party and yearly May Day Fair attract people and dogs from further afield. The latter includes a dog show, so head along to try for a rosette.

walthamforest.gov.uk
Forest Road, E17 5JW
Walthamstow Central tube or rail

There's room for many mutts at this revitalised pub just off Lea Bridge Road roundabout. The enormous interior is divided into several rooms, so the effect is strangely cosy – a feeling enhanced by the junk-shop furniture and offbeat knick-knacks. There's also a sizeable beer garden. An attractive range of drinks is backed by a decent menu of tweaked pub classics, and a choice of roasts on Sunday. In all, it's a mellow place, though dogs will want to avoid the Friday night DJ sessions. Close enough to the marshes for a post-walk pint, and water bowls are available.

claptonhart.com
231 Lower Clapton Road, E5 8EG
Clapton rail

Buy your dog a cake
If you like to celebrate your dog's birthday, then commission a personalised cake from the Hungry Hounds Bakery.
thehungryhoundsbakery.co.uk

Book a training course
Whether you have a new puppy, or an old dog who needs to mend his ways, professional training may be the answer. Louise Glazebrook is a popular trainer in north London.
thedarlingdogcompany.co.uk

Get the beer in
Not actually a beer, it just looks like one. Snuffle beer isn't alcoholic or fizzy, but this mix of beef or chicken with malt barley extracts, vitamin B and so on does come in a beer bottle.
snuffle-dogbeer.com

Commission a photo shoot
Rachel Oates will come to your home or a park (or both) to take photos of your faithful friend over a 2-3-hour session.
racheloatespetphotography.com

Go on a group walk
Meetup has details of all kinds of dog groups, from London Pugs to Single Dog Lovers.
meetup.com

Listen to The Barking Hour
A weekly slot (Thursday afternoons) on BBC Radio London, with much to interest dog-crazy Londoners.

See a film
Keep an eye on *rooftopfilmclub. com* and *wringerandmangle. com* for occasional dog-friendly screenings.

Sign up for agility classes
Mudchute Farm runs regular agility classes for dogs. There's also a 500m agility course in the River Lee Country Park, near Cheshunt.
mudchute.org and *visitleevalley.org.uk*

Take out a subscription
Get a box of goodies delivered every month. Woof Box sends four to six items a month, and features toys, grooming products and healthy treats.
woof-box.co.uk

Try Canicross
Off-road running with your dog. You wear a waist belt, the dog wears a harness, and you're joined by a two-metre bungee line. See Dogfit for information and classes.
dogfit.co.uk

Crate Brewery

EAST LONDON

With more of the green stuff than you'd expect, east London also has
many miles of canal to wander along, not to mention a stretch of the
river Thames. So it may be traffic-clogged in places, but you can always
get away – try Tower Hamlets Cemetery Park for a total change of scene,
or Mudchute Farm, especially if you also have children. Drinking and
dining are a treat here too, whether you're after a historic boozer or a
pimped-up pub. And congratulations to Victoria Park for having two
excellent, though very different, cafés.

Meet other animals at Mudchute City Farm
Revel in the east London countryside

——

Give your dog a trip to the country without leaving Zone 2. Covering 32 acres, this is the most farm-like city farm in London, with fields, woodland, stables and a lot of animals, ranging from pigs to llamas. Dogs need to be on a lead, but can romp off-lead at Millwall Park next door. Mudchute Kitchen (closed Mondays) is dog and family-friendly. Reasonably priced food – beans on toast, tuna mayo sandwiches and a range of fry-ups and pasta dishes – is served inside and out. The café runs a Pet of the Month competition – dogs naturally dominate the winners' photo wall. Contact Mudchute for details of dog agility lessons.

mudchute.org
Pier Street, E14 3HP
Crossharbour or Mudchute DLR

Book a table at Rochelle Canteen
Delicious food in an unlikely Shoreditch setting

——

Ring the bell for admittance to this secluded lunchtime restaurant, hidden behind the wall of a converted Victorian school. Dogs are welcome inside the unfussy, modern room (a converted bike shed), or at one of the courtyard tables (weather permitting). The menu changes daily; dishes are simple but spot-on (fish stew followed by meringue, rhubarb and cream, for example). The canteen isn't licensed; bring your own bottle for £6.50 corkage.

arnoldandhenderson.com
Rochelle School, Arnold Circus, E2 7ES
Shoreditch High Street rail

Mudchute City Farm

MY DOG
Debora Robertson

Every Sunday morning, I head to Columbia Road Flower Market with my husband Séan and our dog, Barney.

I get there as early as possible to avoid the crowds, so I banish bleary eyes with a strong cup of coffee from the cart in Ezra Court, then we're ready to launch ourselves into the melee.

There's been a flower market in this corner of east London since the Nineteenth Century and it's constantly evolving. The street is now lined with smart shops, galleries and cafés (including Hiro & Wolf at no.146, purveyor of chic dog leads and collars, hiro-and-wolf.com), but the main event remains the ravishing market stalls selling cut flowers and plants.

I always start at Mick and Sylvia Grover's herb stall. They've had a pitch on the market for over 40 years and there's nothing they don't know. They always save a Rich Tea biscuit for Barney, so he's under their stall quicker than you can say 'greedy piglet'.

Next, it's Stuart Crump's orchid stall. Other market-goers often look a little startled at his hollered greeting of 'Where's killer?', before they realise he's referring to a 10-year-old border terrier with biscuit crumbs in his beard.

These days, Barney is one dog among many. Columbia Road has become quite the doggy fashion parade. From Great Danes to French Bulldogs, it's a festival of wet noses and shiny coats among the flowers.

www.columbiaroad.info 8am ish until about 2pm ish, every Sunday morning

Join the Breakfast Club

A relaxed diner on the edge of the Olympic Park

——

This canal-side branch of the Breakfast Club is an ideal brunch venue for you and your pooch. Staff are laid-back, there's plenty of room and the furniture is unscuffable. Even better are the outdoor tables and deckchairs – a tempting prospect on sunny days. The menu is no-nonsense, US-tinged comfort food: breakfasts, diner dishes, big sandwiches and wraps; drinks include cocktails and Camden beer. It's the perfect spot before or after a walk, and if the Breakfast Club is full, you can dip into one of the other options on this newly minted restaurant row.

thebreakfastclubcafes.com
29 East Bay Lane, E15 2GW
Hackney Wick rail

Experience Old Spitalfields Market without the crowds

Go on a Thursday for the antiques market

——

The weekends may be too crowded for comfort, but at the Thursday antiques market there's breathing space. The only hazard to navigate is the territorial nature of some of the traders' dogs – otherwise, you and your pooch can spend a couple of happy hours browsing the alluring mix of furniture, prints, ceramics, glass, clothes, records and ephemera, before refuelling at one of the food stalls. Prices are reasonable, there's lots of tempting stock and the atmosphere is easy-going.

oldspitalfieldsmarket.com
Commercial Street, E1 6BG
Liverpool Street tube or rail, or Shoreditch High Street rail

Pitch up at People's Park Tavern

There's a lot going on at this Victoria Park venue

———

A huge barn of a pub, filled with battered furniture and comfortable sofas, with a big Astro-turfed beer garden that leads directly off Victoria Park. It's aimed at 20- and 30-somethings – there are DJs playing on Friday and Saturday nights (dogs: avoid!), crazy golf, a barbecue pit in summer, cocktails and a long list of modish beers (some brewed here). Dogs get water in their bowls and are part of a happy mix that includes families, cyclists and park escapees. The rule is: no children after 7pm; dogs welcome anytime.

peoplesparktavern.pub
360 Victoria Park Road, E9 7BT
Homerton rail

Ramble round Tower Hamlets Cemetery Park

An unexpectedly wild area in E3

———

A lovely, bosky, overgrown patch, with lots of wonderful smells for dogs. As the name suggests, much of the park is a cemetery (one of the 'Magnificent Seven' Victorian cemeteries) and is in the process of being reclaimed by the Friends of Tower Hamlets Cemetery Park. There are also some open, sunny spaces with rough-cut grass, lots of wildflowers and well-established trees, ponds and a few works of art. The park is big enough for a decent walk, but the Ackroyd Drive Green Link joins it to Mile End Park if you want to carry on wandering.

fothcp.org
Southern Grove, E3 4PX
Bow Road or Mile End tube

People's Park Tavern

biscuiteers.com
Dog biscuit treats, including personalised ones if you really want to spoil the mutt. (Remember, he can't actually read.)

charleychau.com
Gorgeous beds and blankets, including the signature Snuggle bed, plus made-to-order leather collars.

countryhounddogboutique.co.uk
Collars, outfits (including a wax jacket), toys and beds, designed for the London dog dreaming of a rural life.

dogsandhorses.co.uk
Classic leather collars, leads and harnesses in subtle colours. Based in London.

eastendbestfriend.com
Handmade toys, accessories and blankets – the bandanas are especially appealing.

hindquarters.com
Tough but stylish beds, leads and collars. The vibe is very much 'less is more'.

hiroandwolf.com
Ethically sourced, these patterned leads and collars pack a visual punch.

houndsofeden.co.uk
Handsome collars, handmade from Harris tweed wool and Liberty print cotton.

rubyrufus.com
One hundred per cent cashmere sweaters and snoods, both plain and patterned.

urbanpoochboutique.com
Everything from a Balmoral check tweed coat to a leopard-print lead. Based in Northumberland.

Welcome the Hounds of Bow
The East End gets a new dog emporium

———

Opened in summer 2016, the Hounds of Bow is the epitome of a modern dog store. Natural and organic food is to the fore, with a big freezer full of raw food, and treats from the likes of Innocent Hound (venison chipolatas, no less). Red Dingo pet adventure leads and collars hang alongside Pet Head grooming products and squeaky toys from Outward Hound. There's also a good choice of dog puzzles. Customers are given a warm welcome, and advice is freely given.

houndsofbow.co.uk
347 Roman Road, E3 5QR
Mile End tube

Kick back at the Kenton
A hound-loving hostelry in Homerton

———

A quirky, Norwegian-run hostelry (the pub sign depicts an elk's head), a short walk from Well Common. Hounds are made very welcome – by customers as well as management – and there are water bowls to hand. Dogs may be able to nab a few titbits from the Beast Feast menu; meatballs in gravy and a steak sandwich are typical, but there are veggie options too, and the chips are top-notch. Sit in the little beer garden, or sink into a bashed-up armchair and contemplate the decor – the walls hold everything from skateboards to framed posters.

kentonpub.co.uk
38 Kenton Road, E9 7AB
Homerton rail

Set your sights at the Marksman
First-class food near Columbia Road
——

Both pints and cocktails are adeptly served at this sensitively modernised Victorian boozer. The wood-panelled ground-floor bar is a cosy spot, complete with handsome vinyl jukebox; there's also an upstairs dining room designed in a more current style, but dogs aren't allowed there. Food is taken seriously here, from the bar snacks (anchovy toast or gubeen cheese, apple jam and oat crackers) to superior Sunday roasts, but you can just pop in for a glass of wine and some spicy peanuts. Handy for a restorative lunch (served long into the afternoon) after the hurly-burly of Columbia Road Flower market. The dog-friendly ground floor has tables for walk-ins.

marksmanpublichouse.com
254 Hackney Road, E2 7SJ
Hoxton rail

Walk the Thames Path to the Grapes
Take in a historic riverside drinking spot
——

Explore the section of the Thames Path that runs from the Tower of London to Limehouse, and finish with a drink at the Grapes. If a patch of grass is needed, there are little parks along the route: Ropemakers Field is the one closest to the pub. Push open the door and you'll be greeted by a clean white dog bowl just inside the entrance. If you're lucky, there will be room to squeeze on to the wooden deck at the back, which overlooks a broad sweep of the Thames (the view includes an Antony Gormley sculpture poking out of the water just outside the pub). If not, the ground-floor bar is a cosy spot for a pint and a stack of whitebait.

thegrapes.co.uk
EC3N to 76 Narrow Street, E14 8BP
Tower Hill tube and Westferry DLR

Make new friends at the Crate Brewery

A sociable hub in Hackney Wick

———

Meet hipster dogs and their owners at this beer and pizza joint on the Lea Navigation canal. As befits industrial-looking Hackney Wick, the decor is rough and ready (bare light bulbs, a bar made from old railway sleepers), the thin crust pizza is good (top picks are prosciutto or veggie star-turn courgette, feta, red onion and gremolata) and the beer choice wide (not only their own brews but carefully sourced buy-ins too). The tables beside the towpath are great for people- and dog-watching, and on sunny days this is the last word in gritty urban conviviality.

cratebrewery.com
The White Building, Queens Yard, E9 5EN
Hackney Wick rail

Crate Brewery

Victoria Park

There's something for everyone in Victoria Park

Visit the 'lungs of east London'

A classic inner London park, with a boating lake, flower gardens, play areas and a skatepark. Dogs can look at these features, but not touch – instead, they have acres of running-around space, or the option of a sedate walk along a relatively quiet stretch of canal. The two park cafés are better than the norm, offering good food and coffee. The Park Café (next to the skatepark) allows dogs on leads inside and serves Indian dishes, such as masala fried eggs and chicken sheekh kebab, alongside toast with jam and interesting smoothies. The Pavilion Café (next to the lake, no dogs inside) has masses of outdoor seats with a view over the water and serves a fine brunch. There are also lots of pro-dog pubs nearby (The Crown, Royal Inn on the Park, People's Park Tavern), so there's plenty of choice. Before you leave, look out for the stone Dogs of Alcibiades flanking the Bonner Gate entrance.

towerhamlets.gov.uk
Grove Road, E3 5TB
Bethnal Green or Mile End tube, or Cambridge Heath or Hackney Wick rail

Maison Dog

SOUTH EAST LONDON

Dogs will love the variety of walk possibilities in south east London, from mysterious Nunhead Cemetery to ancient Oxleas Wood, and people will appreciate the views too – you can see for miles from these hilly locations. The area is also home to the 40-mile Green Chain walk, which links many of these open spaces – it's divided into sections, and is a good project for a fit dog. Back on tarmac, Bermondsey Street is second to none in its pooch appreciation, and there are plenty of neighbourly coffee stops and pubs elsewhere too.

Bask in the welcome at the Greenwich Union

Explore the beer list at this brew pub

———

'We welcome dogs with open arms,' says the barman, and the warmth of the greeting sums up the ethos of the Union. Young bar staff rush around serving well-made, crowd-pleasing dishes (croque monsieur and chips, mussels in a beer sauce, Sunday roasts) to a mix of locals and tourists; they also make sure dogs have water bowls. Hounds can loll in the garden at the back, or tuck into booths in the cosy interior. This was the Meantime Brewing Company's first pub, and real beer is still at the heart of the operation. A staggering choice includes lagers, pale ales, porters, trappist beers, wheat beers and ciders. A fine destination after a romp in Greenwich Park.

greenwichunion.com
56 Royal Hill, SE10 8RT
Greenwich rail

Celebrate the existence of Oxleas Wood

A fabulous green space, sporadically threatened by road development

———

A very special place for a dog walk, Oxleas Wood is at least 8,000 years old in places, covers around 180 acres and offers amazing views. The terrain varies from shaded ancient woodland, dominated by oak trees and thick with brambles, to open meadowland – a dog can get properly muddy here, and it's a useful place to come for shade in the summer months. There are lots of birds, including parakeets, plus squirrels to (unsuccessfully) chase. The park café is not dog-friendly, but the tearoom at Severndroog Castle (a recently restored tower folly) is. If you've set your heart on a slice of home-made cake, check their opening times carefully. Both the Green Chain and the Capital Ring walks go through the woods, if you fancy an even longer hike.

royalgreenwich.gov.uk
Crown Woods Lane, SE18 3JA
Falconwood rail

Oxleas Wood

Run up and down in Greenwich Park

It's easy to get away from the crowds in this Royal Park

——

The amazing views are what makes this park so special – and the climb up to the amazing views will keep you and your hound fit. Away from the tourist hubbub around the Royal Observatory there are plenty of quiet areas, including flower gardens and a herb garden; best of all are the acres of grassy space. Anyone with an over-eager dog will be reassured that the small herd of red and fallow deer is fenced off in the Wilderness, an area in the south east of the park. There are two cafés, and a coffee and snack kiosk – dog owners and their charges have to sit outside. If you're not local, arrive the fun way, by using the Thames Clipper (dogs travel free, but must be on a lead).

royalparks.org.uk
Greenwich Park, SE10 8QY
Cutty Sark DLR

Have a roll in the grass in Brockwell Park

There's a lot of fun to be had in these 126 acres

——

Lovely Brockwell Park, with its varied habitats and wide open spaces, is a joy for owner and dog. Although there are manicured areas and fenced-off lakes, it's really quite rural in feel, with long grass – even a meadow near the Brockwell Gate entrance – for springers to spring in, and plenty of short grass for any dog to roll in. The hilly terrain means lots of views, and the park has some magnificent trees – 25 different types, in fact. Lambeth Country Show, held here every summer, features sheep dog displays; there's also an annual dog show. The park café is housed in 200-year-old Brockwell Hall; dogs are allowed on the beautifully sited terrace. Just outside the Herne Hill entrance you'll find the Florence gastropub and Parlour café, both very welcoming to thirsty hounds.

lambeth.gov.uk
Norwood Road, SE24 9BJ
Herne Hill rail

Go for a stroll round Peckham Rye Common and Park

There's a bit of everything at this neighbourhood gem

——

An ideal combination of lots of open space to play fetch in, and a variety of shadier nooks and crannies, including a wooded area, to investigate. There are a few spots where dogs aren't welcome, or have to be on a lead, but mostly hounds aren't restricted. It's a sociable, neighbourhood kind of park – an easy place in which to meet up with other dog walkers. Pooches aren't allowed inside the park café, but there's plenty of outside seating, treats are sold and water is provided. Lerryn's on Rye Lane is our pick of the coffee stops near the park, while booze hounds should head towards the Ivy House on the Nunhead side of the park.

southwark.gov.uk
Peckham Rye, SE15
Peckham Rye rail

Peckham Rye Common and Park

Ask the staff at Holly & Lil
A great source of merchandise and information

Best known for their handmade leather dog collars – the range is vast, and new ones are introduced seasonally – H&L sells lots of other stuff too. The small shop is crammed with goodies – it's unlikely you'll leave empty handed. Harnesses, leads, bags, beds, bowls, outfits and toys – you name it, they've got it. There are cards and mugs for humans, and hampers and alpaca jumpers for dogs. Pop in for local tips too; they've created a map of the immediate area, showing green spaces and dog-friendly establishments, all with 'paw ratings'. Grooming is offered nearby at 90 Tower Bridge Road, SE1 4TP.

hollyandlil.co.uk
103 Bermondsey Street, SE1 3XB
London Bridge tube or rail

Go on the Green Chain Walk
Travel from Sydenham Wells Park to Horniman Gardens

———

South London has lots of lovely green spaces, but the joy of this stretch of the Green Chain Walk is the variety. Start at Sydenham Wells Park, a well-tended municipal delight, with flower beds and ponds, then follow the Green Chain signs to Sydenham Hill Wood. Here you'll find ancient trees, bluebells and snowdrops, and a variety of birds. Over-excitable dogs will need to be on a lead – the wildlife has priority. At this point, you can head to Horniman Gardens or Dulwich Wood. Snack options are limited – brunch, courtesy of La Petite Bouchée's vintage Citroën van in Sydenham Wells Park, must be booked in advance. The Wood House pub, handily situated between the park and the wood on Sydenham Hill, or the café in Horniman Gardens allow for more spontaneity.

greenchain.com
SE26 to SE23
Sydenham or Sydenham Hill rail and Forest Hill rail

Have a pint alfresco at the Hare & Billet
Make the most of the views at this Blackheath hostelry

———

You can enjoy a pint stretched out on the grass thanks to the Hare & Billet: drinkers are encouraged to sun themselves on the heath, as long as their drinks are in plastic glasses. Slightly off the main drag, the pub is less blighted by traffic than some of Blackheath's pubs, but walking here is still the stress-free option. The interior is modernised, unfussy rustic, with big wooden tables and chairs; the food is decent pub grub. There's a great range of drinks – everything from Pimm's to pints (a rotating range, including some from small local breweries); dogs get a water bowl just inside the main entrance.

hareandbillet.com
1A Hare and Billet Road, SE3 0QJ
Blackheath rail

Make a day of it on Bermondsey Street

Check out the other dogs in SE1

——

A strong contender for the title of the most dog-friendly street in London. With its limited traffic and mix of welcoming shops, cafés and pubs, Bermondsey Street is a great place for a Saturday amble. Almost everywhere is happy to see your dog: stand-outs include José (a classy tapas bar), the Woolpack (a pub with a beer garden out back) and Hej (an airy Swedish coffee house on Bermondsey Square, just past dog-friendly Bermonsey Square hotel). Green spaces – Leathermarket Gardens, Tanner Street Park, the grounds of St Mary Magdalen church – are close at hand if you need time out. More tips can be had from lovely pet store Holly & Lil; staff know the area inside out. For a longer excursion, add on Maltby Street market just a few minutes' walk away – the Ropewalk itself might be a bit too crowded for dog comfort, but the surrounding streets (Druid Street, Spa Road) have food and bric-a-brac outlets too. And if you needed any further persuasion about the area's credentials, the Bermondsey Street Festival, held in September, encourages dogs to attend – and to come in costume.

Bermondsey Street, SE1
London Bridge tube or rail

Maison Dog

Be tempted by Maison Dog
A well-curated shop for urbane hounds
——

Enter the wonderful world of Westow House
A warm welcome awaits at this Crystal Palace boozer
——

A delightful shop, offering grooming, accessories and collectibles, including a fine display of antique dog paintings. (There's also a rail of second-hand women's clothes.) It's all very East Dulwich, and charming to boot, with designs for dog beds and cushions, greetings cards and mugs that you won't have seen elsewhere. There's a range of hand-made dogs bowls, some smart leads and collars, and even home-made dog food. Also offered are puppy socialisation classes; owners enjoy a glass of prosecco while the pups mingle.

maisondoglondon.com
20 Northcross Road, SE15 5AR
East Dulwich rail

The big glass jar of dog treats ('Scooby snacks- help yourself') and the stack of water bowls means no-one ever has to ask if dogs are welcome here. Westow House is just across the road from Crystal Palace park, and is spacious enough for a pack of Great Danes and shabby enough for the muddiest pup. After some park action, sink down into one of the sofas, with a real ale and a welsh rarebit. There are books galore, board games, and a pub quiz on Tuesdays. The only drawback? The outside space looks directly on to a busy junction.

westowhouse.com
79 Westow Hill, SE19 1TX
Crystal Palace rail

Drink up at Ivy House
Support a community enterprise

———

The jar of dog biscuits on the bar is just one indication of the all-inclusive spirit of this pub. It's London's first co-operatively owned pub, and aims to be much more than a regular boozer, with lots of events (there's a small stage in the back room), a quiz, chess and knitting clubs, and pre-school children's sessions. Beers come from a wide range of London breweries, including the nearby Brockley Brewing Company; food is smart pub grub. Come here after exploring Nunhead Cemetery, and cosy down in the charming 1930s front bar, or head round the back to the beer garden, which is decked out with bunting and lots of container plants. The Ivy House is the focus of much local love, and deservedly so.

ivyhousenunhead.com
40 Stuart Road, SE15 3BE
Nunhead rail

Lose yourself in Nunhead Cemetery
One of the 'Magnificent Seven' London cemeteries

———

An intriguing, beautiful ramble for humans, but one that dogs will probably remember for the scent of foxes. The cemetery is a beguiling mix of open, formal walkways and overgrown paths, filled with crumbling memorials in heavily wooded areas as well as a few modern graves on carefully tended lawns. The 52 acres allow plenty of space to get lost in, and the tranquility makes it feel a long way from central London – though you can see St Paul's from a (legally protected) viewpoint. Prepare for dogs off-lead to get muddy, even in summer.

southwark.gov.uk
Linden Grove, SE15
Nunhead rail

TOP TEN

Beer gardens for big dogs

The Brownswood Tavern, *Clissold Park*
'Dogs of all sizes and breeds welcome' at this N4 favourite. There's outdoor seating for 150 people. *thebrownswood.co.uk*

The Canonbury Tavern, *Canonbury*
A spacious pub with a huge garden – it's well-maintained and refined, just like the neighbourhood. *thecanonbury.co.uk*

Pub on the Park, *London Fields*
Not so much a beer garden, more a huge deck overlooking the park – good for 20-somethings and their pooches. *pubonthepark.com*

The Coach & Horses, *Barnes*
An unfussy vibe means dogs and children can relax in this long, ramshackle beer garden just off the High Street. *coachandhorsesbarnes.co.uk*

The Princess of Wales, *Clapton*
Pizza, craft beer and a prime location on the canal – outdoor tables look out over the water. *princessofwalesclapton.co.uk*

The Roebuck, *Chiswick*
A lovely walled space, with flowers and greenery. Dogs get toys, treats and water. *foodandfuel.co.uk*

Royal Inn on the Park, *Victoria Park*
Bang next to the park – perfect for a post-walk pint. *royalinnonthepark.com*

The Station Hotel, *Hither Green*
The Station Hotel is dog-friendly throughout, but its very urban garden allows room for even more pooches in summer. *stationhotelhithergreen.co.uk*

Stein's, *Richmond*
Continental beer garden on the riverside, serving German beer and food. Weekends only in winter. *stein-s.com*

The Wood House, *Sydenham*
The expansive patio space is ringed by trees and a set of (heated) garden huts. They've also found room for a burger shack. *thewoodhousedulwich.co.uk*

Kennington Park

SOUTH LONDON

The very urban nature and dense housing of much of south London means the parks and green spaces are cherished, and it's a good place for sociable pups and owners. You won't find hills, but otherwise there's plenty for dogs to enjoy, together with attractive pubs and coffee houses for parched people. Most idiosyncratic is the Tea House Theatre café on the edge of Vauxhall Pleasure Gardens – a lovely antidote to the identikit high rises shooting up in this part of the city.

Green Room

Enjoy the good vibes at the Green Room
A handy pit stop for South Bank walks
——

This light, airy brasserie is the result of a collaboration between the National Theatre and local social-enterprise group Coin Street Community Builders. Unlike many South Bank eateries, they're delighted to see dogs (check out their A-board) – and the slightly spartan nature of the interior means no one (dog or child) worries about making a mess. A crowd-pleasing, ethically sourced menu has burgers (including a vegan option), chilli, salads and small plates; drinks run from coffee to Meantime beer on tap. A further plus is the small garden out front – grab a deckchair and enjoy.

www.greenroom.london
101 Upper Ground, SE1 9PP
Waterloo tube or rail

Bound along to Battersea Park
A civilised spot just south of the Thames

——

Battersea Park has something for every dog, including the possibility of a Thames-side stroll. The 200-acre site has amazing trees, open spaces, lots of birds and wildlife, and a lake. Humans will also like the sculptures (not only Nicola Hicks' Brown Dog, but work by Barbara Hepworth and Henry Moore too), the Peace Pagoda and the Festival of Britain remnants. The Tea Terrace kiosk is a magnet for dog walkers – hot drinks and snacks can be consumed under trees or on the terrace; a small marquee offers a little protection from the elements. Dogs are also welcome inside and out at the Italian café at Putt in the Park. Staff are friendly, they serve great coffee (the place is licensed too), and breakfast items such as sausage sandwiches are followed by delicious wood-fired pizzas.

batterseapark.org
Albert Bridge Road, SW11 4NJ
Battersea Park rail

Pay a visit to Archie and Agnes
A one-stop shop in Stockwell

——

Pop in for a smart collar, a squeaky toy or some organic food, and get happily distracted by the antics of the doggy day care crew – separate from the shop, but clearly visible. Stock is a carefully curated selection of beds, toys and accessories by UK names such as Mutts & Hounds, Lily's Kitchen and Hiro + Wolf. Archie and Agnes also has a grooming salon.

archieandagnes.com
89 Landor Road, SW9 9RT
Clapham North tube or Clapham High Street rail

TOP TEN
Dog groomers

Barking Betty, *Battersea*
BB covers a swathe of south London, offering boarding, walking, day care, and a range of grooming services.
barkingbetty.com

Bishops Bark, *Fulham*
Grooming, day care, plus a range of classy dog food, accessories and toys. And yes, it is near Bishop's Park.
bishopsbark.com

Chiswick Park Pet Spa & Boutique, *Chiswick*
You can see the dogs being groomed here, and there are sessions for nervous pets as well as all the usual services.
chiswickparkpetspa.co.uk

Clarendon Cross Canines, *Holland Park*
A family-run business with a loyal following for its grooming services. There's a shop and day care too.
canines.cc

Greenwich Hound, *Greenwich*
The full spa session here includes a pawdicure … but you can also just book a swift wash-and-go groom. Day care is also available.
greenwich-hound.com

Groom Dog City, *Bethnal Green*
Anything from a wash to a full trim – or go creative with one of their non-toxic dyes. Book a Sunday session and explore Columbia Road market while you wait.
groomdogcity.com

Richmond Rascals, *Richmond*
The choice of treatments here goes from standard to pedicures and nail painting. There's also a pet shop, plus walking, day care and boarding.
richmondrascals.com

Sniffles Dog Grooming Spa, *Hampstead*
All the services you'd expect, including 'furcuts', are available at this savvy groomers. Day care and walking are offered too.
sniffles-spa.co.uk

The Pet Spa, *Fulham*
An upmarket groomer for very indulged pets – treatments include massages and one-hour pedicures. The Spa also runs a model agency, so if you feel your pooch has star potential, get in touch.
petspalondon.com

Purple Bone, *Notting Hill*
A smart, modern salon offering everything from a full groom to a straightforward wash and dry. There are branches in Westfield and Chelsea too.
purplebone.com

Take refuge in Brunswick House
A bright spot in built-up Vauxhall
——

An incongruous sight amid the high rises, traffic gyratory system and Vauxhall bus station, eighteenth-century Brunswick House is a fun, sophisticated spot for a coffee or a cocktail. The bar and terrace welcome pups; the restaurant is off-limits, but you can order substantial snacks such as sausage with mustard, or cheese and crackers. Make time for a rummage through the LASSCO architectural salvage if you're here during the daytime. Handy for river walks too.

brunswickhouse.co
30 Wandsworth Road, SW8 2LG
Vauxhall tube or rail

Settle in at the Three Stags
Relaxed drinking and dining opposite the Imperial War Museum
——

The Three Stags might look like an average boozer from the outside, but the food offering is a cut above. Pizzas are made on the first floor (evenings only); the ground-floor bar serves pub classics made with care and attention – the fish finger sandwich comes stuffed with real fish in batter, for example. There's an easy-going atmosphere, and pups fit right in; it's the pub of choice for many local dog owners. Check out the Timorous Beasties London-themed wallpaper while you're there.

thethreestags.london
67–69 Kennington Road, SE1 7PZ
Lambeth North tube

The Three Stags

Applaud the Tea House Theatre

A quirky café overlooking Vauxhall Pleasure Gardens

—

'Muddy boots and dogs are welcome' says the sign on the door, giving the measure of this generously spirited café and venue. Newspapers and magazines are provided, as are toys, books and board games; customers settle down in armchairs, or sit at wooden tables decorated with fresh flowers. There's a substantial menu of teas, from a mug of builder's to specialist brews, plus cooked breakfasts and main dishes such as game stew or a gourmet burger. Cake comes in giant slices. Tables outside overlook Vauxhall Pleasure Gardens, a community-minded green space ideal for a short walk.

teahousetheatre.co.uk
139 Vauxhall Walk, SE11 5HL
Vauxhall tube or rail

Set a course for the Lighthouse

Canine customers welcome at this Battersea boozer

—

A popular, refurbished local with nice staff and a jolly beer garden, where dogs are welcome throughout. Pub grub is served alongside a range of drinks that includes plenty of real ales. The beer garden has a few covered huts, as well as heaters for chilly nights. Settle in to watch the football, play a board game or get your breath back after a game of fetch in nearby Battersea Park.

thelighthousebattersea.com
441 Battersea Park Road, SW11 4LR
Battersea Park or Clapham Junction rail

TOP TEN
Blogs and websites

barkarama.co.uk
Good for stylish
dog merchandise
recommendations.

borrowmydoggy.com
The site matches owners
with dog lovers who are
happy to help with walks,
day care and holiday cover.

fourandsons.com
A dog-centric culture and
lifestyle magazine and website;
it's Australian-based but has
a world view.

libertylondongirl.com
Popular lifestyle blogger with
a miniature dachshund.

londondogforum.co.uk
Everything from walks
to dog health and welfare
is covered.

manaboutadogblog.
wordpress.com
Engaging, south east
London-centric reviews
of places to eat, drink and
stay with a hound.

packdog.com
Beautifully curated photos
of dogs, divided by breed.
Add your dog, or simply
live vicariously.

petspyjamas.com
A huge directory of dog
accessories and dog-friendly
places to stay, plus useful
info (a guide to the pet
passport scheme,
for example).

styletails.com
'Design and lifestyle trends
for modern pet owners' – this
is where to source the latest
collar, pick up a recipe for
dog treats or gawp at photos
of chic pooches.

thedogvine.com
Home of the London dog
blog as well as a directory of
events and (some) services.

Appreciate the beer gardens at the Avalon
A crowd-pleasing pub close to Clapham Common

———

One of a small company of pro-dog south London pubs, the Avalon is an impressive set-up. The tiled interior is a nicely lit, handsome space, with room for dining and drinking, but it's the outdoor areas that make it special. There's a terrace out front, a partially covered courtyard (with TV) to one side, and (weekends and evenings, weather permitting) a large, spruced-up beer garden out the back. Enjoy burgers and pizzas there, or a more gastropub menu inside – wherever you go, the mutt can come too. Naturally, there are dog treats and water bowls on hand.

theavalonlondon.com
16 Balham Hill, SW12 9EB
Clapham South tube, or Vauxhall tube or rail

Unwind at the Fentiman Arms
Catch this all-rounder just behind the Oval

———

The Fentiman caters to everyone: food-focused but happy to serve a sausage roll or Scotch egg; it has a fire in winter and a well-kept beer garden in summer; and though it's dog-friendly throughout, two cats occupy prime sun-worshipping spots. If you opt for a meal at one of the dining tables, Fido can come too. It's handily placed for Vauxhall Park, a little further along Fentiman Road.

thefentimanarms.co.uk
64 Fentiman Road, SW8 1LA
Oval tube

Meet up in Kennington Park
Mingle at this sociable south London park

———

Kennington Park packs a lot into a compact site – there are playgrounds and lots of sports facilities, as well as open parkland and formal gardens – and is a godsend for local dog walkers. Dogs on leads are welcome in most areas – even the charming, old-fashioned flower garden – but there are two off-lead dog exercise areas too. The Arts and Crafts-style park café is the place to meet up for an (outdoor) cuppa, while the Sugar Pot (just across Kennington Park Road) serves good coffee and allows hounds inside.

kenningtonpark.org
Kennington Park Road, SE11 4BE
Oval tube

Kennington Park

Lavish Habit

Develop a Lavish Habit
A sunny-natured café and shop in Balham

———

Dogs are valued customers at this artfully distressed café/shop – and they're a handsome bunch too in this gentrified corner of Balham. We spotted a beautifully trimmed Scottie next to the quirky stock who looked like part of the display. It's a gift-hunter's dream, with everything from jewellery to homewares – and who wouldn't want an eggcup in the shape of a pug? A welcoming vibe, Monmouth coffee and an appealing menu – breakfasts, toasties, salads, cakes – keep humans happy. Before you leave, check out the garden at the back.

lavishhabit.co.uk
75 Bedford Hill, SW12 9HA
Balham tube or rail

Stretch four legs on Clapham Common
The epitome of an inner London park

———

What the Common lacks in variety it makes up for in size, with most of the 200 or so acres taken up by grassland. Dogs off-lead need to be obedient here – the park is crisscrossed by roads. Apart from the sheer space, the park's plus points are the Long Pond (fun for water-loving hounds), Italian café La Baita (a popular meeting place for dog walkers) and the Windmill (a dog-friendly Young's pub that backs on to the Common).

lambeth.gov.uk
Clapham Common, SW4
Clapham Common or Clapham South tube

Richmond

SOUTH WEST LONDON

Dogs can pretend they're in the countryside round here, with Richmond Park providing the most space for roaming – though the rural life means that owners need to watch out for wildlife, from swans on the riverside to deer in the park. There are great day trips to be had in south west London: not only Richmond Park, but along the Thames, as well as Wimbledon Common; and all have amiable pubs and tea rooms geared to a doggy clientele, none more so than Paws for Coffee near Bushy Park.

Run free on Wimbledon Common
Watch out for golf balls in SW19

—

Huge, bounding hounds are made happy by the endless acres on Wimbledon Common. There's masses of space – and you can walk on to Putney Heath if the mood takes you. The mix includes ponds, woodland and heath, plus a golf club (there's a public right of way through the course). There's also a windmill, behind which is the Windmill Tearooms – good for basic meals and mugs of tea; dogs outside only. The Crooked Billet and Hand in Hand are next to each other at the southern end of the common; both are big, dog-friendly pubs, and are happy to provide plastic glasses for drinking on the grass. Be aware of restrictions in certain areas during bird-nesting season.

wpcc.org.uk
SW19
Southfields tube, or Wimbledon tube or rail

Get closer to Wandsworth Common
Tails wag at this cherished local park

—

The Common may not be the largest local space, but it's much loved by park users. It's got a bit of everything, for a start – lakes, wooded areas, open grassy spaces, contained sections away from the road, not to mention the scent of foxes and tantalising glimpses of squirrels. Try the trim trail jumps too – built for humans, they're great for agile hounds. The Common is also beautifully maintained, with plenty of dog bins and very little litter. The likeable park café, the Skylark, is a further plus.

wandsworth.gov.uk
SW11 and SW18
Wandsworth Common rail

Wandsworth Common

Tide Tables café

Refuel at the Tide Tables or Hollyhock cafés
Perfect post-walk perches near the river in Richmond

———

These sister cafés are two of the best-placed eateries in Richmond. Tide Tables is in a converted arch underneath Richmond Bridge, while Hollyhock has a charming lookout up in Terrace Gardens. Both serve uncomplicated vegetarian dishes in generous portions, as well as cakes, hot drinks, juices and smoothies. Blankets are provided so that you can enjoy the views of the river for as long as possible – but everyone and their pooch is welcome inside too; dog bowls are provided.

tidetablescafe.com
Tide Tables café, 2 the Arches, TW9 1TH
Hollyhock café, Terrace Gardens, TW10 6UX
Richmond tube or rail

Chow down at Henry Root
Fulham brasserie with a fondness for dogs

—

Dogs rule as far as this smart neighbourhood brasserie is concerned. Not only does Henry Root put on occasional Dog's Dinners (the Wimbledon-themed one encouraged canines to come in their best tennis whites), but hounds are made a fuss of from breakfast through to dinner. Water and biscuits can be provided. Humans get a crowd-pleasing roster of brunch dishes, salads, burgers and steaks, backed by a lengthy drinks list (cocktails included). The Fulham location means staff are probably not expecting any really mucky pups through the door.

thehenryroot.com
9 Park Walk, SW10 0AJ
14 bus, Gloucester Road or South Kensington tube, or West Brompton rail

Hunker down at the Hope
An easy-going Wandsworth Common stalwart

—

Dogs of all sizes are allowed everywhere, inside and out, at the Hope, and the pub gets a lot of customers straight after their Wandsworth Common walk. (The Capital Ring walk also passes the pub.) You can take drinks back into the park in plastic cups, hunker down inside with a burger and a pint, or soak up the sun at the outdoor tables. The interior has been modernised, but this remains a pub, with a quiz night, a TV and real ale. Inevitably, weekends can get hectic.

thehopepub.co.uk
1 Bellevue Road, SW17 7EG
Wandsworth Common rail

Stock up at Pet Pavilion
Make an afternoon of it in Chelsea
—

If you can't find it in Pet Pavilion, then Fido probably doesn't need it. The shop is stuffed with all manner of foodstuffs, grooming products, leads, collars, toys and accessories, not to mention a towering stack of beds. Staff are knowledgeable and personable – and there's every likelihood that your four-legged shopping companion will get a dog treat (Pet Pavilion make their own range, including baked chicken and gravy bones flavour). There are branches in Kensington, Notting Hill and Wimbledon, too – grooming is offered at every outlet.

petpavilion.co.uk
Chelsea Farmers Market, 125 Sydney Street, SW3 6NR
Sloane Square or South Kensington tube

Walk to lunch at Petersham Nurseries
Forget the city pavements for a few hours
—

Walk along the towpath, on the north side of the Thames from either Richmond or Twickenham, diverting for a run-around in Marble Hill Park before crossing the river on Hammertons ferry (adults £1, dogs go free). Then it's a short stroll alongside pretty Petersham Meadows to Petersham Nurseries, where the bucolic feel continues. Potter around the outdoor plant displays, or investigate the upmarket home and garden wares. Simple lunches or tea and cake can be had in the Teahouse (there's a smart restaurant too), which has tables in a beautiful old glasshouse and dotted around outdoors. Better than a trip to the country, and the hound is welcome pretty much everywhere.

petershamnurseries.com
Church Lane, off Petersham Road, TW10 7AB
Richmond tube or rail, or Twickenham rail

Petersham Nurseries

White Swan

Get close to the river at the White Swan
Kick back beside the Thames at Twickenham

This stretch of the river path is dog-walking bliss, and it's made even better by the presence of the historic White Swan. Pop in for anything from a pint of London Pride to a Sunday roast with Yorkshire puddings. The outdoor tables are in a garden bang next to the Thames; it's idyllic when the suns shines, but under water at very high tides (you'll get plenty of warning). There's an easy-going vibe, and a good contingent of dogs.

whiteswantwickenham.co.uk
Riverside, TW1 3DN
Twickenham rail

Mingle with dogs and children at Skylark Café

Pretty-as-a-picture café on Wandsworth Common

—

More ambitious than most park cafés, Skylark has coffee from Caravan Roastery and cakes from Dee Light in Balham, to name just two of their classy suppliers. It's both canine- and child-friendly, so dogs are required to be on leads but can go anywhere, either the cheery interior or at the many trestle tables outside. There are treats near the till and water on hand. Humans can order breakfast, brunch and lunch, or opt for the sweet stuff: lamingtons, wheat-free carrot cake, scones with strawberry jam or Jude's ice-cream. Deservedly popular with the locals.

skylarkcafe.co.uk
Dorlcote Road, SW18 3RT
Wandsworth Common rail

Meet Bushy Park pups at Paws for Coffee

Terrible pun, lovely café

—

Step over the resting dogs to place your order at this charming café. Across the road from Bushy Park, it's aimed at dog walkers and their charges, but is pretty child-friendly too. There are calves' hooves and home-made dog treats (cheese and chicken, fishy delights) on the menu, plus a puppychino (warm goat's milk with bits of black pudding). Humans get breakfasts (the café opens at 8am during the week, 9am weekends), sandwiches, salads, an array of cakes and Italian ice-cream. The community noticeboard is full of dog-related specialists and events, notably the Hounds of the Hill dog show.

41 High Street, TW12 1NB
Fulwell or Hampton rail

Revel in the grandeur
of Richmond Park
*Walk for miles in a beautiful and
varied landscape*

——

The biggest enclosed space in London, Richmond Park can feel gloriously like the countryside, with big stretches of heathland and ancient trees. The wilder nature of the park brings issues, though. The red and fallow deer that roam freely can feel threatened by dogs, even at quite a distance, and every year there are incidents where either a dog or a deer comes off badly from an encounter (and no one wants the YouTube ignominy of a Fenton-style incident). The Royal Parks' advice is that you avoid the park completely during birthing (May–June) and rutting (September–October) seasons, or at least keep your dog on a lead and near the edges of the park. Owners should also be aware that there's a risk of Lyme disease, so check your dog for ticks. Hounds are allowed almost everywhere apart from formal areas, such as the Isabella Plantation. There are cafés and pubs aplenty in Richmond, as well as two cafés and two 'refreshment points' in the park.

royalparks.org.uk
TW10
Richmond tube or rail, or North Sheen rail

Richmond Park

TOP TEN

More parks – outer London

Alexandra Park, *N22*
Panoramic views make this a popular park, but there's plenty of space for all (196 acres).

Bostall Heath & Woods, *SE2*
A bit of a south east London secret; together, the heath and woods provide 390 acres of dog-walking pleasure.

Bushy Park, *Hampton*
The second-largest Royal Park, Bushy has woods, grassland, ponds and great vistas, but watch out for the deer.

Crystal Palace Park, *SE19*
Hills, wooded areas and lots of grass – and a set of dinosaur sculptures around a lake.

Fryent Country Park, *NW9*
Woods, ponds and more than 250 acres of hilly open space to romp in.

Gunnersbury Park, *W3*
In need of some TLC, but still a winning combination of landscaped gardens and wide open spaces.

Morden Hall Park, *Morden*
A National Trust park that encourages dog walking. The 120-acre site includes the river Wandle, meadows and wetlands.

Osterly Park, *Isleworth*
Dogs are allowed in the park (and can be off lead in the long grass areas), but not in the NT-owned house and formal garden.

Trent Country Park, *Enfield*
Pretend you're not in London at this 413-acre park, and enjoy a long walk through meadows and ancient woodland.

Wanstead Flats, *E11*
As the name suggest, no hills here, just acres of grass and Jubilee Pond.

Dine at the Harwood Arms
Feasting in Fulham

———

There aren't many places with a Michelin star and a dog bowl, but happily the Harwood Arms has both. It's a pub too – you can drop in for a pint and a posh bar snack, and sit by the fire with your four-legged friend. But it's all too tempting to book for a special meal. Mention the beast when you book, and expect the likes of Cornish sea bass with jersey royals, samphire, smoked eel and sorrel.

harwoodarms.com
Walham Grove, SW6 1QP
Fulham Broadway tube

Live the rural dream in Barnes Village
There's everything a dog could need in SW13

———

Barnes is the ideal spot for a city dog who yearns to be a country hound. Life in this leafy corner seems to revolve around dogs: there are water bowls outside everything from hairdressers to homeware stores, not one but two pet shops (the Barnes Pet Shop on Church Road, and Pets Corner on Barnes High Street), classy butcher's shops and lots of welcoming hostelries. From the Brown Dog gastropub to the trad Coach and Horses, there are dogs wherever you go. The Saturday farmer's market is great for mingling, and for walks there's the riverside or Barnes Common.

SW13
Barnes Bridge rail

Southwold

OUT OF TOWN

London is wonderful, but every once in a while a dog needs some country air or a sea breeze. Try one of these day trips – or make a weekend of it – for a hassle-free, dog-friendly outing. If your hound has never splashed in the sea or run on a sandy beach, or smelled a real wood, then you're both in for a treat.

Leigh-on-Sea, Essex

Just 40 minutes from Fenchurch Street

—

Southend's more refined sibling, Leigh-on-Sea offers shoreline, parkland and relaxed town-centre mooching. The train drops you close to the pretty cockle sheds and shingle of the estuary; stop at one of the sheds for a seafood snack or full-blown fish and chip feast, or continue along the coastal path if you need to get Fido away from scavenging temptation. To get to the heart of town, walk uphill; Leigh Road and the Broadway have a good mix of independent shops and cafés, most of them happy to see your pooch. More vigorous walks can be had in Two Tree Island Nature Reserve (just south of the station; dogs need to be on a lead or under strict supervision) or in Belfairs Wood (to the north of the town). There's a folk festival every June, with plenty of outdoor stages.

Hindhead and the Devil's Punch Bowl, Surrey

Take in the far-reaching views

—

Since the Hindhead Tunnel was built in 2011, what was the old A3 is now a sweeping path that skirts the hollow of the Devil's Punch Bowl. It's perfect for dog walking, and has wonderful views. If you want a longer walk, there are trails criss-crossing the National Trust land, including the long-distance Greensand Way. The terrain is a mixture of heath and woodland, with amazing purple heather in season. Keep an eye out for Highland cattle (NT advice is to let your dog off the lead if livestock approach you). The café next to the car park has lots of outside seating (no dogs inside) and water bowls. Note that you won't necessarily get a phone signal on this walk, so if you're planning to stray off a marked trail, take an Ordnance Survey map with you.

TOP TEN
Dog-friendly sleepovers

Albion House, *Ramsgate, Kent*
Dogs under 12kg can check into this modish seaside establishment in up-and-coming Ramsgate. Choose between beach or cliff walks – both are delightful.
albionhouseramsgate.co.uk

Bailiffscourt Hotel & Spa, *Climping, West Sussex*
The faux-medieval hotel set in 30 landscaped acres on the coast looks grand, but the vibe is relaxed. Investigate their Sandy Paws deal.
hshotels.co.uk

Crown & Castle, *Orford, Suffolk*
They really care about dogs at this food-focused bolthole. Pups stay in one of the Garden rooms, and are welcome in the bar – or book the doggie table in the restaurant.
crownandcastle.co.uk

Dundas Arms, *Kintbury, Berkshire*
A chichi pub-hotel, with a good food offering. Dogs are 'warmly welcome', and it's ideally-placed for river and canal walks.
dundasarms.co.uk

Gallivant, *Camber, East Sussex*
A scamper away from the magnificent beach and dunes, the Gallivant is an upmarket beach 'motel' where Fido doesn't have to pay a supplement.
thegallivant.co.uk

Hotel Felix, *Cambridge*
A smart, canine-friendly hotel, with grounds for romping in. Dogs are allowed in the Orangery and Terrace dining and drinking areas – only the posh restaurant is off-bounds.
hotelfelix.co.uk

Kingham Plough, *Kingham, Oxfordshire*
Canine customers have to dine in the bar, but that's pretty much the only restriction at this Cotswold bolthole.
hekinghamplough.co.uk

Lygon Arms, *Broadway, Worcestershire*
A dog-loving hotel in a dog-loving town. Check out the Four-Legged Friends package.
lygonarmshotel.co.uk

The Ship, *Dunwich, Suffolk*
A lovely, old-fashioned pub with rooms. Dunwich beach is open to dogs year-round, but there's also the pub garden and nearby heathland to play in.
www.shipatdunwich.co.uk

Victoria Inn, *Holkham, Norfolk*
Worth the drive for glorious Holkham beach, a short walk from the Victoria. Dogs are welcome in 10 of the 20 rooms, and in the bar/restaurant.
www.holkham.co.uk/victoria

Burnham Beeches, Buckinghamshire

Explore 540 acres of glorious woodland

———

The City of London owns and maintains this magnificent site. The ancient woodland contains trees that are hundreds of years old, with Druid's Oak being the oldest living tree here at more than 800 years – it's now supported by cables. A variety of walking trails runs through the woods, from mile-long treks for lazy dogs to the five-mile Historical Trail, but there's plenty of open space and opportunities for wandering at will, too. Note that in parts of Burnham Beeches dogs must be on a lead, and that a section of the Beeches Café is a dog-free zone. The Blackwood Arms in nearby Littleworth Common is the nearest dog-friendly pub.

Littlehampton West Beach and Climping Beach, West Sussex

Scamper along the sand all year round

———

A mix of dunes, shingle and – when the tide is out – expanses of sand are an alluring mix for a dog. What's more, there are no restrictions on dogs at any time of year (unlike East Beach, just across the river Arun), and you can walk all the way along to the next beach, Climping (also unrestricted access). Here, you'll find Climping Beach Café and, in Climping village, the Black Horse Inn; both welcome dogs. Or you could have a slap-up tea at the Bailiffscourt Hotel. West Beach also has the basic West Beach Café. If you really want to see the bright lights of Littlehampton East Beach, your only option from May to September (when dogs are banned there) is to walk the pooch on the promenade.

Hastings

Hastings, East Sussex
Possibly the most dog-friendly town on the south coast

Dogs pretty much get an access-all-areas pass in Hastings. Most establishments, particularly in the scenic Old Town and long stretches of the pebbly beach, are open to them. Stop for a coffee or a light lunch at Petit Fi café, or while away the afternoon at the Crown gastropub. There are real ales and an open fire at the FILO (First In Last Out), or vodka shots and stellar Sunday lunches at the Dragon Bar. The antique and bric-a-brac shops are used to dogs inspecting their wares – there's even outdoor browsing at the Yard. Hastings Country Park provides acres of running-around space and great views out to sea, and is bang next to the Old Town; access it via steps or the East Hill Cliff Railway. Or you could walk along the prom, past the new pier, to St Leonards-on-Sea (only half a mile) for more dog-loving pubs, cafés and shops. Wherever you wander, be prepared for lots of doggy interaction.

Whitstable, Kent
Seafood-centred town that's perfect for a doggy day trip
—

Southwold, Suffolk
A very civilised seaside break
—

The shingle beach is open to dogs all year round here – though some areas have lead-only rules in high season. After a romp, repair to the Old Neptune pub – very dog-friendly, and right on the beach. In town, the Black Dog (real ales) is happily pro-pup, as are the Twelve Taps (gins and craft beers) and the bar (not the restaurant) at the Duke of Cumberland (Sunday-afternoon music sessions). Dogs can go into many of the shops and cafés too – Windy Corner Stores and Café is a treasured example – though just wandering the pretty streets while window-shopping is a popular activity too. For green space, wander through Whitstable Castle Gardens; for a sensory overload, check out the fish markets area around the harbour.

A genteel resort, with delis, boutiques and upmarket eateries, and a super dog-friendly one. Hounds are welcome at the Harbour Inn and at the Lord Nelson; both serve good food and Adnams (the town brewery) beer. If the weather is favourable, there are plenty of classy takeaway options – fish and chips included (try Mrs T's Fish & Chips near the harbour). The handsome restored pier is a must; enjoy the views, but don't miss the mechanical games at the Under the Pier Show (especially the rent-a-dog experience). There are water bowls on and around the pier, and the café is open to all comers. The southern stretch of Southwold beach is open to dogs year-round, while the main beach is off-limits May to September. A little rowing-boat ferry can transport you and your furry friend across the river Blyth to Walberswick, for yet more walks and pubs. The ferry runs from late March to the end of October; people pay £1, dogs travel for free.

TOP TEN
Country walks near London

Ashdown Forest, *Kent*
A mix of woodland and heath, covering 20 square miles of land. Livestock graze in certain areas – check locations at the Forest Centre if you want to avoid them.
ashdownforest.org

Ashridge Estate, *Hertfordshire*
Come for views across the Chilterns and 80 miles of footpaths, through woods, chalk downlands and meadows.
nationaltrust.org.uk

Box Hill, *Surrey*
Box Hill offers a series of trails, from a gentle meander to an eight-mile hike, all with lovely views.
nationaltrust.org.uk

Coombe Hill, *Buckinghamshire*
The highest point in the Chilterns. Walk on grass and heathland and blow the cobwebs away.
nationaltrust.org.uk

Cuckmere Haven, *East Sussex*
You can admire the scenery – the beach is next to the Seven Sisters cliffs – while your pooch scampers on the beach all year round.
visiteastbourne.com

Hastings Country Park, *East Sussex*
Walk on sandstone cliffs covered with grass, gorse and trees, and enjoy the amazing sea views.
hastings.gov.uk

Stour Valley Path, *Suffolk*
The section of the long distance walk near Dedham Vale and Flatford Mill is easy walking, often alongside the river.
dedhamvalestourvalley.org

Thames Path, *Berkshire*
Goring to Pangbourne is a pretty stretch of the Thames path, with hills on either side of the flat river walk.
nationaltrail.co.uk

Thorpeness, *Suffolk*
Hounds can romp on this shingle beach year-round, then you can both wander round the quaint village of Thorpeness.
visit-aldeburgh.co.uk

Winkworth Arboretum, *Surrey*
National Trust-owned land with more than 1,000 different trees and shrubs, a lake, and a variety of trails (some hilly). Dogs on leads only.
nationaltrust.org.uk

Windsor Great Park, Berkshire
Enjoy a majestic stroll

———

The 4,800-acre park is prime dog-walking territory, with great views at every turn. Wander at will, or follow the Long Walk, a three-mile path that runs from Windsor Castle to the Copper Horse statue. Watch out for red deer (there are around 500 of them), and note that throughout much of the park, dogs need to be kept on leads. Picnics are encouraged, but otherwise the Fox & Hounds (near Bishopsgate) is a good place to refuel (booking advisable if you want to eat), with barbecues on summer weekends, water bowls and a warm welcome. Keen walkers and eager dogs can continue striding on through the park towards Virginia Water.

Sheffield Park and Garden, East Sussex
New flora and fauna to explore and smell

———

Beautiful in all seasons, Sheffield Park is described by the National Trust as 'a horticultural work of art' and is particularly stunning in autumn. There are four lakes and a waterfall, and a vast collection of trees and shrubs in the landscaped gardens, plus 250 acres of open space in the parkland. Dogs are allowed into the formal gardens after 1.30pm daily; they have to be on a short lead (these are available at reception if you don't have one). Hounds have the run of the East Park section of the parkland at any time. You can picnic anywhere, and there's also the Coach House tearoom (where dogs are permitted in the garden room). Drinking water is available. A fun way to visit is to get the train to East Grinstead and then hop on the Bluebell steam railway (£2 per dog).

INDEX

*Thanks to everyone who came on a walk, passed on advice or helped in any way,
particularly Sally Adams, Patricia Ambrose, Sheba and Simon Cassini, Lisa Clough,
Sophie Gardiner, Ruth Jarvis, Karl Jefferies, Daisy Malivoire, Cath Phillips,
Chris Pierre, Ben Rowe, Julie and Laura Savage, Ros Sales, Craig Sheppard,
Rose and Graham White, Geoff Wilson and Yolanda Zappaterra.*

1 3 5 7 9 10 8 6 4 2

Ebury Press, an imprint of Ebury Publishing,
20 Vauxhall Bridge Road, London, SW1V 2SA

Ebury Press is part of the Penguin Random House
group of companies whose addresses can be found
at global.penguinrandomhouse.com

Penguin
Random House
UK

Text by Sarah Guy © Ebury Press 2017
Photography © Ben Rowe 2017

First published by Ebury Press in April 2017

www.penguin.co.uk

A CIP catalogue record for this book is available
from the British Library

Design: Linda Lundin
Photography page 20: Locanda Locatelli
Photography page 42: Henrietta Morrison
Photography page 88: Séan Donnellan
Photography page 101: Daisy Malivoire
Photography page 148: Chris Pierre
All other photography: Ben Rowe

ISBN: 978-1-785-03511-1

Orginated by Born Group, London
Printed and bound in China by RR Donnelley

Penguin Random House is committed to a
sustainable future for our business, our readers
and our planet. This book is made from Forest
Stewardship Council® certified paper.

MIX
Paper from
responsible sources
FSC
www.fsc.org   FSC® C018179